the DANCING FATHER

DISCOVER JOY
AND POWER
THROUGH A DAILY
RELATIONSHIP
WITH GOD

BRIAN KINSEY

www.BrianKinsey.com

©2016 by Brian Kinsey

©2016 Dust Jacket Press
The Dancing Father: Discover Joy and Power Through A Daily Relationship With God / Brian Kinsey

ISBN: 978-1-943140-80-0

All rights reserved. No part of this publication may be reproduced, distributed, or transmitted in any form or by any means, including photocopying, recording, or other electronic or mechanical methods, without the prior written permission of the publisher, except in the case of brief quotations embodied in critical reviews and certain other noncommercial uses permitted by copyright law. For permission requests, write to the publisher, addressed at the address below:

Dust Jacket Press
P.O. Box 721243
Oklahoma City, OK 73172
www.dustjacket.com

Ordering information for print editions:
Quantity sales. Special discounts are available on quantity purchases by corporations, associations, and others. For details, check out at www.BrianKinsey.com.

Individual sales. Dust Jacket Press publications are available through most bookstores. They can also be ordered directly from Dust Jacket: Tel: (800) 495-0192; Email: info@dustjacket; www.dustjacket.com

Dust Jacket logos are registered trademarks of Dust Jacket Press, Inc.

All Scripture quotations, unless otherwise indicated, are taken from THE HOLY BIBLE, KING JAMES VERSION.

Scripture quotations marked " NIV" are taken from the Holy Bible, New International Version® NIV®. Copyright ©1973, 1978, 1984, 2011 by Biblica, Inc. Used by permission of Zondervan. All rights reserved worldwide. www.zondervan.com. The " NIV" and "New International Version" are trademarks registered in the United States Patent and Trademark Office by Biblica, Inc.

Scripture quotations marked (NLT) are taken from the Holy Bible, New Living Translation, copyright © 1996, 2004, 2007 by Tyndale House Foundation. Used by permission of Tyndale House Publishers, Inc., Carol Stream, Illinois 60188. All rights reserved.

Lord of the Dance Words: Sydney Carter
©1963 Stainer & Bell, Ltd. (Admin. Hope Publishing Company, Carol Stream,
IL 60188). All rights reserved. Used by permission. Reprinted under license #78220

Print License - License No. FBL-A003190
1. AND THE FATHER WILL DANCE
Words adapted from Zephaniah 3:14 and Psalm 32:2,4, Music by Mark Hayes
© Copyright 1984 Hinshaw Music (administered worldwide by Fred Bock Music Co., Inc.)
All rights reserved. Used by Permission.

Song ID: 64885
Song Title: Amazed
Writer(s): Jared Anderson
Label Company:
Copyright © 2003 Integrity Worship Music (ASCAP)(adm. at CapitolCMGPublishing.com) All rights reserved. Used by permission.

Cover & Interior Design: D.E. West / Dust Jacket Creative Services

Printed in the United States of America

www.BrianKinsey.com

DEDICATION

Dedicated to my wonderful Children, Grandchildren and Sons-in-law.

To my beautiful first-born daughter, Lisa. I marvel at your walk with God, your careful love of your two children, Dylan & Kinsey, and your husband Bryan. I dance over you with great joy because you became what I envisioned for your life: a devoted mother, a loving wife and powerful witness for Jesus. Let's continue the dance.

To my lovely and wonderful daughter Dana, the spark in my life that gives me hope for a better tomorrow, and whose unquenchable faith has caused my heart to dance. Now that you and Daniel and the 3 munchkins, Noah, Eva and Ella have joined us in ministry, may our dance continue until the sunset of my life.

To my smart and industrious son Lee, who earned a PhD and established a successful counseling practice before age 29, I salute your tremendous purpose driven life and dance over you with joy.

AND THE FATHER WILL DANCE

By Mark Hayes
Adapted from Zephaniah 3:14–17 and Psalm 34:2–4

And the Father will dance over you in joy!
He will take delight in whom He loves.
Is that a choir I hear singing the praises of God?
No, the Lord God Himself is exulting over you in song!
And He will joy over you in song.
And He will joy over you in song.

My soul will make its boast in God,
For He has answered all my cries.
His faithfulness to me is as sure as the dawn of a new day.

Awake my soul! Awake my soul! Awake my soul and sing!
Let my spirit rejoice, Let my spirit rejoice, Let my spirit rejoice in God.
Sing O daughter of Zion with all your heart.
Cast away fear for you have been restored.
Put on the garment of praise as on a festival day.

Join with the Father in glorious, jubilant song.
And He will joy over you in song.
And He will joy over you in song.

And the Father will dance over you in joy.
He will take delight in whom He loves.
Is that a choir I hear singing the praises of God?
No, the Lord God Himself is exulting over you in song!
God rejoices over you.
God rejoices over you.
God rejoices over you in song.

CONTENTS

Dedication iii
And the Father will Dance..v
Foreword..ix
An Invitation to Dance xi

Part I: Dancing Lessons 1
   Lesson 1: Trust the God Who Loves You 3
   Lesson 2: Follow God's Direction 13
   Lesson 3: Follow God's Way 21
   Lesson 4: Stick with It 29

Part II: The Dance of Delight 39
   Step 1: Seek a Relationship with the Father 41
   Step 2: Pray without Ceasing... 59
   Step 3: Remain Constant.. 79
   Step 4: Come into Agreement 101
   Step 5: Find Joy in the Midst of Battle............................. 121
   Step 6: Praise at All Times 143
   Step 7: Love the Truth 165

Afterword... 185

FOREWORD

The title itself is gripping. Just think, to have the Father Himself tap you on the shoulder and say, "Break from whatever you are doing. This dance is mine!"

It is simply a re-discovery of the joy and power found through a daily relationship with God. Every chapter ends with "Your next move . . ." Waltzing through trust, slow-dancing through following, the embrace of "stick with it" – on and on I could go. This is Brian Kinsey at his best.

Power comes out of relationship. The book is filled with power points! The very statement, "If thou be the Son of God…" tells us that hell hears what heaven says about you. There's nothing hell fears any more than the power of the sonship relationship.

Read this book to be blessed. Ingest it to be strengthened. As much as anything, dance with the Father with joy – for "the joy of the Lord is our strength!"

I commend Brian Kinsey for this most unique approach to building a relationship with the Father. So, dance on! Through it all, you are in His arms.

~ T. F. Tenney

AN INVITATION TO DANCE

This book has grown from two great desires of my heart. The first is my constant passion to increase the effectiveness of the ministry to which God has called me. I have a deep hunger to see souls saved and saints receive a greater measure of grace so they are equipped to tackle the unique problems of our society. I have been preaching since I was eleven years of age, and the passage of time has only increased my passion to see the Holy Ghost work in me and through me. My life's journey has been to know God more intimately and be used by God more exhaustively. Through that seeking, God has led me to seven principles in Scripture that have truly transformed my ministry. As I have learned to faithfully apply these concepts to my life and work, I have seen dramatically greater results from my preaching and pastoral work. I take no credit for this. It is the work of the Spirit through—and sometimes in spite of—my humble efforts. As I have been able to apply these biblical principles to my life, the Spirit has had greater freedom and has produced a greater harvest.

Therefore my first purpose in sharing these principles is to encourage God's shepherds and to strengthen and bless the flock. In God's economy, the most important factor is the condition of one's heart. God can do far more with a prepared vessel than with a prepared message. Effective ministry depends on having both a renewed spirit and a renewed mind working together to produce

God's purpose. I offer this book in the hope of strengthening pastors, teachers, missionaries, and Christian leaders in all capacities.

A second burning desire leads me to write this book. Over the years, I have been grieved by the degree to which God's saints are tossed to and fro by the winds of emotion, excitement, temporary joy, and false passion. Far too often, believers seek God only through sensational, mountaintop experiences, the kind that produce great fervor. Like Peter on the Mount of Transfiguration, these zealous souls mistake the momentary thrill of a spiritual high for the disciplined constancy of an ongoing relationship with God. As a result, they run from conference to conference, revival meeting to revival meeting, and even church to church, seeking the ecstatic feeling they have mistaken for a deep relationship with the Father. The result is a chaotic spirituality at best. At worst, this continual seeking of excitement leads to frustration with God and the abandonment of faith. This breaks my heart.

Therefore my second motive for writing is to offer a pathway to spiritual maturity that avoids both the false buoyancy and the needless disappointments that come from chasing one euphoric experience after another. The seven spiritual principles described in this book lead to a spiritual life on the level plain. Having gained this spiritual maturity, we are able to welcome the moments when God chooses to reveal himself through rapturous experience without clinging so tightly to them that we plunge to the depths when the feeling inevitably slips away. Our life with God can be, and should be, a daily delight and not a dreary monotony punctuated only occasionally by brilliant sunshine.

This book is arranged in two parts. Part I is a series of four lessons that will prepare you for the dance of delight with your heavenly Father. These are the foundational concepts that you must master if you are to have any meaningful contact with the Father. These are the underlying principles, the "music," we might say, that accompanies your daily relationship with God. Part II describes the dance of delight you will enjoy with your heavenly Father. These seven steps, or moves, are the actions you take to enter into a consistent daily interaction with the Father. Each action springs from a divine principle of the spiritual life. As you consistently practice these seven actions, you will find your relationship with the Father growing deeper, stronger, and more precious than ever before.

Of course, the valuable principles in this book will be useless to you unless you find practical ways to put them into practice in your daily life. Each chapter of this book includes a section titled "Your Next Move," which is designed to help you do exactly that. Whether you read this book by yourself in a single sitting or study it with a group of others over several weeks, do not neglect this section! As you discipline yourself to put these principles into action, you will find the Dance of Delight with your heavenly Father becomes second nature. You will move beyond understanding what God wants from you to entering into the blessing of a rich daily fellowship with Him.

I offer this work in the hope that it will lead you to discover a deeper, healthier, more constant relationship with your heavenly Father, who dances with joy at the very sight of you. I pray that your soul may dance in return.

PART 1
Dancing Lessons

LESSON 1
Trust the God Who Loves You

The purpose of this book is to help you discover a pathway to spirituality that leads to a mature, growing, joy-filled, and daily relationship with God. By learning to apply the seven spiritual principles described here, you will come to see and welcome the delight of your heavenly Father in ways that now elude you. You will become more faithful, more confident of your relationship with God, and you will be used by him to a far greater degree than you had previously imagined. These seven principles will enable you to escape the mediocrity of mere religious exercise and bring the wonderful experience of God home with you.

However, before you can benefit from these life-transforming discoveries, it is essential that you make a few choices that will enable you to apply what you are learning. These decisions are prerequisites for your spiritual growth. Without them, you could learn every spiritual principle in Scripture and still not budge in your spiritual life. Think of it this way. If you were to consult an athletic trainer for advice on getting in better shape, that trainer could teach you quite a bit. She could assess your current condition, give you advice on improving your diet, and show you the workouts that would benefit you most in gaining strength, losing weight, and improving your cardiovascular system. You would know all you needed to know to become healthier. But unless you had made a prior commitment to pursue good health, that knowledge wouldn't benefit you one bit. To get in better physical condition, you must first commit yourself to the goal of getting healthy. You must choose to alter your daily routines to include exercise. You to have give up certain foods from your diet and add others. Without those foundational choices, seeking advice from a trainer will do no more for your health than standing on your head. You might understand what she had to say and even agree; but without those prior commitments you would never benefit from the trainer's advice.

In the same way, you must set some things in place before you can benefit from sound spiritual teaching. These are prerequisites to spiritual growth. And the first one is this: To experience a relationship with God, you must learn to trust the God who loves you. Your concept of God will set the course for your relationship with Him. If you view God as a stern, angry judge who is eager to punish you, your relationship with Him will always be negative. You will avoid seeking God, hiding in shame and fear. However, if you are able to gain a correct view of God, seeing Him as a loving father who takes delight in you, His child, you will have a positive, healthy, intimate relationship with your heavenly Father. To grow spiritually, you must learn to trust the God who loves you.

GOD LOVES YOU

Your heavenly Father delights in you. God loves you, and He rejoices over you. That's a new concept for many Christians. Over the years we have developed a mental image of God that is anything but delightful. Perhaps this is because we have heard so much preaching about sin and judgment that we cannot imagine God as a happy, inviting person. We know God hates sin, and we know we are sinful people. It stands to reason that God would be more displeased with us than delighted, doesn't it?

To the extent that many of us think of God as a father at all, we picture Him as a stern disciplinarian. He is a parent with extremely high expectations, no tolerance for failure, and an aversion to smiling. God is like the teacher you can never please or the coach you can never impress. When you bring home a report card with straight A's, this version of God harrumphs and says, "Is that the best you could do?" We picture God as being annoyed, displeased, or even angry with us. At the very best, He tolerates us. Is He ever delighted with us? Probably not. Sadly, that is the concept of God many of us carry around in our heads.

Not surprisingly, that mental picture of God casts a pall over our spiritual lives. We see ourselves as the naughty child who can never do anything right. On those rare occasions when we do sense God's presence and blessing, we hold onto that feeling for dear life, hoping the mountaintop experience will never end. It always does, of course. Afterward, we feel even more lonely and abandoned than before. "What happened?" we wonder. "Was it something I did? Has God decided that I'm no longer lovable? Do I need to do something to get that relationship back?"

This sad, lonely experience leads us to pull all the harder at God's sleeve, begging for attention. We eagerly sign up for the next seminar. We attend the gospel concert with great expectations that God will meet us there. We run from peak to valley to peak again, desperately seeking that feeling of being blessed, filled, and at peace with God. It is an exhausting way to live, and it takes a tremendous toll on our spiritual lives. Few children can maintain a relationship with an earthly father who is cold, distant, and only occasionally bestows his affection. No one can develop a healthy relationship with a heavenly Father who withholds or bestows His love based on the whim of a moment.

That is why it is vital that you hear this and fully understand it: Your heavenly Father delights in you. He loves you. And He wants much more than fleeting moments of connection with you. He longs for a constant relationship in which you both take delight. When you finally understand that God takes great pleasure in your relationship with Him, it will be like finding a treasure. Just think, God enjoys being around you! He wants to be near you!

When you experience this healthy, joy-filled connection with God, your spiritual life and your ministry will take giant steps forward. No longer will you seek God only in the heights of spiritual fervor; you will experience His daily presence as well. You will encounter fewer spiritual valleys, and you will find them less frustrating because you know that your heavenly Father is still there, still loves you, and is eager to have communion with you again very soon.

THE DANCING FATHER

Have you ever asked the question: "What does God really want from me, and for me?" Many of us assume that the main thing God wants for us is that we behave well, and what He wants from us is that we go to church, pay our tithes, and volunteer to serve. Those things are good and important, but simply being good and going to church—either as a duty or as a form of entertainment—is not what pleases God. What He really wants is a relationship with each one of us. Just as a parent longs to love and be loved by his or her child, so God desires a close relationship with each of us. Yet how do we have that relationship? If that's what God most wants, how does it come about?

We are essentially asking the same question that King David asked in 1 Chronicles 13:12: "How shall I bring the ark of God home to me?" In other words, how can I bring the presence and power of God into my personal life, into my home, my school, my job? When you discover the answer to that question, you will understand that you are destined for something more than running from one conference or service to another, looking for the latest spiritual fix. Much to your delight, you will find that God has a destiny already decided for you, and that if you will learn from Him the values and qualities He desires, you will become what He wants you to be.

Having been born again of water and of Spirit, baptized in Jesus' name and filled with the Holy Ghost as evidenced by speaking with other tongues, you can rest assured that the adoption papers have been filled out and the process of becoming a member of God's family is complete; you now belong to Him. Our joy in being adopted by God is obvious. We were dead in our trespasses and sins, without hope in the world (Ephesians 2:1, 12), and living in a pitiful condition. This is where God found us, washed us, cleansed us and made us acceptable in His sight. Joy is our natural response to salvation. And what is God's reaction? To answer that question, let's consider a beautiful and surprising image of God offered by one of the most inspiring prophets of the Old Testament, Zephaniah. It is the image of a dancing father.

I first noticed this image in an intriguing statement found in Zephaniah 3:17: "The LORD thy God in the midst of thee is mighty; he will save, he will rejoice over thee with joy; he will rest in his love, he will joy over thee with singing." What really surprised me about that passage was what I learned about the meaning of the word joy as used here. I'd never thought much about it, other than the obvious idea it means happiness. However, the commentator pointed out that the word here translated as joy is a Hebrew word that means "to spin around (under the influence of any violent emotion)."[1] Think about that for a moment: to spin around under the influence of emotion. That sounds a lot like dancing! In fact it is dancing. The prophet tells us that God will be so overcome with delight at the salvation of His people that He will express that joy in motion. He will dance over us!

As I reflected more on the meaning of this passage, I realized that I, too, have danced in that way. You probably have as well. I have danced with joy at the sight of my newborn child. I have leapt in the air and clapped my hands at their first word and first step. I have picked them up in my arms and twirled around with delight. I have danced over my children in joy so full, so boundless that it could not help but find expression through my arms and hands and feet. I think every parent has known the joy of

---

1. James Strong, *A Concise Dictionary of the Words in the Hebrew Bible; With Their Renderings in the Authorized English Version* (Nashville, Tenn.: Abingdon Press, 1890), 27.

dancing with delight over a child. And the Scriptures tells us that God dances with that same joy over us!

Now consider this: Why do we, as earthly parents, dance over our children? What accounts for our exuberant display of emotion? Do we delight in our children because they are perfect? Is it because they contribute to our lives financially? Is it because they have done something rare or astounding? Even as love struck parents, we can admit that our children are not perfect, they are an absolute drain on our finances, and most of the things they do are so ordinary that they would be downright boring if done by someone else's child. The reason we are delighted with our children is simply because they exist—they are our children. A child who enters the world is a reason for joy. Any adoptive parent feels that same thrill at bringing a child into their home. They now have someone to call their own. In essence they are saying, "You belong to me. Now you're mine." Yet even that does not fully describe our joy as parents. We rejoice because of what our children will become. We envision their future, their growth, their learning, their mastery of skills—we imagine them as young men and women growing to maturity, and we are filled with pride and delight and hope.

And this is exactly the joy that God feels about you. You belong to God, and He has a divine plan for your development, improvement, and growth—just as any loving parent would. This is the reason God rejoices over us: We belong to Him, and He enables us to escape the horrible destiny of the world and realize the quality of life He has designed for us. This is a great relief to us, and a great delight to the Father. And He expresses that joy in dancing.

This image of God has been captured beautifully by one of the contemporary songwriters, Jared Anderson, in the song "Amazed."

You dance over me

While I am unaware

You sing all around

But I never hear the sound

Lord, I'm amazed by You

Lord, I'm amazed by You

Lord, I'm amazed by You

How You love me[2]

We can no longer think of God as a judge only, a strict disciplinarian, or an austere, loveless parent. God is our dancing Father! He is a good, loving parent who delights in our presence, desires the best for us, and guides us daily on the pathway to maturity. We can be done with vain searching after spiritual highs and enter a joy-filled journey with our Father. Keep this image firmly in your mind as you move through the pages of this book—and through your life with God. He is your loving parent, your delighted Dad, the dancing Father.

Now that you have a proper vision of God, we can move to the second prerequisite for your spiritual growth. To do that, we must pay a visit to one of the most unusual geographic features in North America, one created not by the hand of God but by an act of Congress. Our next chapter begins with a visit to a tiny pinpoint in the remote desert of the western states.

---
2. Jared Anderson, *"Amazed"* (Brentwood, TN.: Capitol CMG Publishing, 2003). Used by permission. License Number: 583800

YOUR NEXT MOVE

Your next move is to reshape your concept of God to match His actual nature, not your preconceived notions about Him. To do that, try one or more of the following activities.

1. List five words that describe your current concept of God. Beside each word, write a brief explanation for how you arrived at that notion. For example, "Judge—Teaching from parents." Finally, examine the Bible to see whether each description is accurate.

2. Identify the most mature believer you know. Engage that person in brief conversation on the question, "How do you know God loves you?" Tell someone else what you discovered from that experience.

3. Read the Gospel of John. As you do, write down your observations about what God is like. In what ways does this confirm your thinking about God? What surprises you?

LESSON 2
Follow God's Direction

The Colorado Plateau is a rugged, mostly mountainous region in the southwestern United States. This region comprising some one hundred thirty thousand square miles is notable for the unusual geological formations that dot its rugged landscape. Drive west along U.S. Route 164, which roughly bisects the region, and you will encounter scenery that seems inspired by Dr. Seuss. There are spherically shaped protrusions of the earth's surface called domes, reddish chimney shaped rock formations called hoodoos, petrified forests, natural bridges, and slot canyons that measure just a few feet wide at the top but plummet a hundred or more feet to the canyon floor. The Colorado Plateau is home to the Grand Canyon, ten national parks, eighteen national monuments, and some thirty-nine other protected wilderness areas.

However, the oddest feature of this amazing region is truly unique, formed not by rushing floodwaters or howling winds but by the simple stroke of a pen. On February 24, 1863, the U.S. Congress created the Arizona Territory from the western part of the existing New Mexico Territory. The boundary of this new territory was defined not as a particular longitude or latitude, nor along a river. Instead, it as defined as a line running due south from the southwest corner of the Colorado Territory. With that unusual decree, the Congress set in motion the creation of a single point that would become the boundary of four states. Known as the Four Corners, this cartographical oddity marks the junction of Colorado, New Mexico, Arizona, and Utah. If you were to visit the Four Corners Monument, maintained by the Navajo Nation Department of Parks and Recreation at latitude 36° 59' 56.3" west and latitude 109° 02' 42.6" north, you could stand on that exact spot where four political jurisdictions come together at a single point. From there, a step in any direction would, literally, alter your state! That's one place on earth where the slightest change in your direction will dramatically alter your destination.

Your spiritual life is another arena in which a slight change in direction produces a vastly different outcome. Which way are you headed? Choosing the right direction is a key to unlocking God's purpose for your life. God wants you to do more than serve Him at church; He wants to transfer the blessing of worship to your daily life. Emotion is a good thing, a gift from God. But unless we have learned to hear and follow the voice of God, emotion will only lead us to listen to the wrong voices. When your choices reflect the wisdom of God He will dance over you with joy and you will receive "the riches of the glory of His inheritance in his saints" (Ephesians 1:18).

The Bible provides many examples of people who chose to follow God. They set their face toward God and His will for their lives. Each step they took drew them closer to God and His purpose. There are also many examples of people who turned away from God. In at least one case, we find contrasting examples in the same family. Abraham chose to follow God's purpose. Abraham's nephew Lot chose a different goal for himself. Let's look first at his story, which shows how a single step in the wrong direction can derail us from seeking God's purpose.

LOT'S STORY

God had blessed Abraham and his household with material wealth, which, in their ancient society, meant a large number of flocks and herds. As part of Abraham's household, Lot was similarly blessed. The two men had amassed so much livestock that the place they were living was not large enough to contain the abundance. That was a great problem to have! To avoid problems between the two of them, Abraham gave Lot a choice. He said:

> *Let there be no strife, I pray thee, between me and thee, and between my herdmen and thy herdmen; for we be brethren. Is not the whole land before thee? Separate thyself, I pray thee, from me: if thou wilt take the left hand, then I will go to the right; or if thou depart to the right hand, then I will go to the left. And Lot lifted up his eyes, and beheld all the plain of Jordan, that it was well watered every where, before the* Lord *destroyed Sodom and Gomorrah, even as the garden of the* Lord, *like the land of Egypt, as thou comest unto Zoar. Then Lot chose him all the plain of Jordan; and Lot journeyed*

east: and they separated themselves the one from the other. (Genesis 13:8–11)

From a secular viewpoint, Lot made the right choice. He chose the fertile valley and left Abraham with the rough, mountainous country. Lot was a practical man, and positioned himself to succeed as a herdsman and trader. He chose both the better land, which also had the best prospects for developing trade with the people who lived nearby. It was a solid business decision. However, this choice separated Lot from Abraham, the anointed man of God. Lot headed in the wrong direction. He "dwelled in the cities of the plain, and pitched his tent toward Sodom" (Genesis 13:12). Knowing the rest of the story as we do (see Genesis 19), we can see that this choice placed Lot in grave peril and set the tone for the rest of his life.

Separating yourself from God, His Word, and His people is never the right choice. To grow in God's grace and live into the future He has for you, you must set your direction firmly toward God and His purpose for your life. Which way are you facing?

Many Christians today are quietly making a choice similar to the one Lot made. For a variety of reasons, they disconnect themselves from God's Word and His people, just as Lot distanced himself from Abraham. Some do so because they are disappointed with the church, particularly after hearing of the moral failure of a prominent minister or being in disagreement with church leaders or fellow parishioners. Their disappointment causes them to leave the fellowship of the church and its teaching. Others don't consciously choose to change their direction; they simply drift off course. Many things compete for our time and attention, especially on our precious weekends. Sporting events, travel, or countless leisure activities may interrupt their worship. Before long, the habit of weekly worship becomes occasional or sporadic or nonexistent. Still others, like Lot, make the risky decision to pursue opportunities that take them away from the household of faith. They choose business situations, romantic involvements, or other relationships that place them closer to the people of the world than to the people of God.

Despite the frustrations and distractions we may experience in church life, the right choice is always to stay connected to the household of faith and the anointed preachers who speak God's Word as revealed in the Scriptures. God's Word, when rightly divided, will cause spiritual discomfort. Yet we must allow the Spirit's conviction against wrongdoing and selfish living to bring us to repentance and realign us with God's true purpose. Refusal to take this path always ends badly, just as it did for Lot. Only when you are willing to hear and apply the Word of God will you make right decisions for your life.

We are now living in the days the apostle Paul foretold when he said, "For the time will come when they will not endure sound doctrine; but after their own lusts shall they heap to themselves teachers, having itching ears; And they shall turn away their ears from the truth, and shall be turned unto fables" (2 Timothy 4:3–4). When we are willing to hear and apply the Word of God, we will make choices that take us further in the direction God has for us. When we make choices based on our personal preferences and desires, we will move further from God and His agenda for our lives.

Are you willing to base your life on the Word of God? Will you consistently seek God through your own study of the Word, by consistent worship, and by responding to the conviction of the

Holy Spirit? As you do so, you will move further and further in the direction God has chosen for you.

ABRAHAM'S CHOICE

Abraham also made a decision about which direction to face. As soon as Lot separated himself from Abraham, God met with Abraham and offered him a choice, just as Abraham had offered a choice to Lot.

> *And the Lord said unto Abram, after that Lot was separated from him, Lift up now thine eyes, and look from the place where thou art northward, and southward, and eastward, and westward: For all the land which thou seest, to thee will I give it, and to thy seed for ever. And I will make thy seed as the dust of the earth: so that if a man can number the dust of the earth, then shall thy seed also be numbered. Arise, walk through the land in the length of it and in the breadth of it; for I will give it unto thee. Then Abram removed his tent, and came and dwelt in the plain of Mamre, which is in Hebron, and built there an altar unto the Lord. (Genesis 13:14-18)*

Abraham received the privilege of walking through the entire land and choosing the borders of his own promise. In essence, God was saying, "You can choose how big you want the Promised Land to be." Isn't that amazing? God actually let Abraham choose the size of the blessing. Abraham might have been left with rough mountains, but he was headed in the right direction.

What about you? How much of God do you really want? How far do you want to advance in the direction He has chosen for you? How much do you want to grow? How effective do you want your ministry to be? That choice is offered to you, just as it was to Abraham. The only right response to this divine choice is to do as Abram did: "Then Abram removed his tent, and came and dwelt in the plain of Mamre, which is in Hebron, and built there an altar unto the LORD" (Genesis 13:18).

If you really want to grow in the Spirit and receive all that God has for you, you must choose to pursue God through His Word. Remove your tent, walk through the land, and build an altar unto the Lord. In other words, stop going through the motions of religious ritual. Stop seeking any opportunity or desire that points you away from God. Stop trying to reach your own goals under the guise of serving God. Gather for worship and hear the Word of God proclaimed. Drink in the Scriptures through private devotions and group Bible study. Avoid any opportunity, relationship, or situation that might turn you away from God's purpose. Set your course in only one direction—toward God and the future He has for you.

Can you see God dancing over Abraham as he heads in the direction of Hebron? God dances over your right choices too when you choose to move in His direction. Staying connected to the Word of God, regardless of distractions and difficulties, will allow you the privilege of determining how big your Promised Land will be. Build your altar to God daily by staying connected to His Word.

Now that you have chosen the correct view of God, as one who loves you and delights in His relationship with you, and you have chosen the right direction for your life, facing God and His purpose for you, we can move to the third prerequisite for success in your spiritual journey. Our discovery begins on a hot summer night near the end of the last millennium. In the following chapter, we board a small, single-engine plane en route to an island off Cape Cod, Massachusetts.

YOUR NEXT MOVE

Your next move is to commit yourself to following God's ways by discovering His Word. To do that, engage in all of the following activities.

1. Establish the daily spiritual practice of reading and reflecting on God's Word, the Bible.

2. Establish the weekly habit of worship participation at your local church. Make a single decision to go to church—not a weekly yes-or-no choice.

3. Establish a daily prayer time that includes this prayer, "Lord, direct my steps today."

LESSON 3
Follow God's Way

On July 16, 1999, at 8:39 p.m., a Piper Saratoga taxied onto the runway at Essex County Airport in Fairfield, New Jersey. The day had been swelteringly hot, and even then, minutes after sunset, the mercury hovered near 90 degrees. A blanket of warm, wet air shrouded the horizon with haze. The little plane nosed left onto runway 22 to catch the slight southwesterly breeze, and with a final glance at the dashboard gauges, the pilot opened the throttle and released the brakes. The high-performance, single-engine craft sped forward, lifted into the thick night air and disappeared. The pilot had filed a flight plan that would take him and two passengers east, along the Connecticut coastline. They were headed for Martha's Vineyard, an island off the coast of Cape Cod, where the three were to attend a wedding the following day. They never arrived.

At a quarter past two the next morning, family members alerted the Coast Guard that the plane was missing. A rescue operation was mounted at four o'clock and continued for two days, until searchers declared no hope of finding survivors. A research vessel spotted debris from the plane the next day, and on July 20, the fuselage was located on the ocean floor. Divers confirmed that it contained the bodies of the pilot, John F. Kennedy Jr., his wife, Carolyn Bessette, and her sister Lauren.

What caused the crash of this airplane, resulting in the death of the only son of President John F. Kennedy? As investigators pieced together details, the likely answer emerged: pilot error. According to the National Transportation Safety Board, the accident occurred because Kennedy failed "to maintain control of the airplane during a descent over water at night, which was a result of spatial disorientation."[3] Spatial disorientation is a condition in which one cannot determine the position of his or her body in space. It can affect pilots, divers, and even children playing blind man's bluff. In simple terms, someone suffering from spatial disorientation cannot correctly identify which way is up.

Because of the dark night and heavy summer haze blanketing the horizon, visibility was poor. Flying by visual flight rules—that is, without a special license to fly using the plane's instruments alone—was permitted under those conditions but was extremely difficult. Lacking an instrument rating, Kennedy was left to steer by his own sense of direction. When that failed, the plane crashed.

This tragic tale offers a strong caution for airplane pilots and for spiritual travelers. It is possible to have the right intention and the right destination but fail by choosing the wrong attitude. In flying and in spiritual growth, you cannot rely on your own sense of direction. You must be guided by something outside yourself.

---

3. National Transportation Safety Board Office of Public Affairs, *"NTSB releases final report on investigation of crash of aircraft piloted by John F. Kennedy Jr.,"* July 6, 2000, http://www.ntsb.gov/news/pressreleases/Pages/NTSB_NTSB_releases_final_report_on_investigation_of_crash_of_aircraft_piloted_by_John_F_Kennedy_Jr.aspx.

To reach the goal of a daily, constant relationship with God that produces maturity, you must rely fully on God's ways. You must trust God's will, plans, and timing—not your own. To see how this principle plays out in real life, we'll skip a generation and pick up God's story with Abraham's irrepressible grandson, Jacob.

JACOB'S STORY

Jacob was headed in the right direction, but he chose the wrong path to get there. As Abraham's grandson, Jacob was heir to all the promises God had made to Abraham. And Jacob was desperate to receive those promises, so much so that he resorted to swindling his older brother, Esau, out of his lawful birthright and tricking their father, Isaac, into passing the promised blessing to him instead. A short time later, Jacob was forced to leave home, fleeing from the wrath of his brother. Jacob came to a place called Bethel (called Luz at that time), and he "tarried there all night, because the sun was set" (Genesis 28:11). During the night, God visited Jacob in a vision, showing him a ladder of access to the heavens, with angels ascending and descending upon it. There, God promised Jacob the same blessing and protection that He had promised to Abraham. It would seem that Jacob's wish to have a right relationship with God was finally fulfilled, but it wasn't.

Jacob's life was marked by struggle and frustration. He labored for years, never coming one step closer to the blessing God had promised. How was that possible? Jacob had the right goal—he was pursuing God's purpose. And God had promised to give the blessing to Jacob. The problem was that Jacob's attitude was wrong. He chose God's purpose, but he was unwilling to trust God's ways. Jacob sought God's blessing through his own means. When Jacob left Bethel after his vision, the Bible says he "went on *his* journey, and came into the land of the people of the east" (Genesis 29:1, emphasis added). Jacob was pursuing God's direction, but he was doing it in his way. In dealing with his brother and father, Jacob relied on deceit. By laboring seven years for the hand of his beloved Rachel, Jacob was counting on his own strength and determination. Through years of wrangling with his father-in-law and employer, Laban, Jacob made use of cunning. The one thing Jacob was unwilling to do was trust God to provide His blessing in His way. As a result, Jacob's life was a struggle. In fact, he was later renamed Israel, which means "he struggles with God" (Genesis 32:28). His story is proof that it is possible to have the right destination in mind but choose the wrong means to get there. When you do that, you'll never arrive.

The long night that began at Bethel didn't end for Jacob until some twenty years later. For two decades he struggled to obtain God's promises using his own cunning, strength, and skill. At the end of that time, he was essentially at odds with everyone he knew. Having worn out his welcome with his father-in-law, Laban, Jacob was forced to flee back to Canaan and the uncertain welcome he would receive from Esau. Just prior to meeting up with Esau, Jacob spent the night at a ford on the river Jabbok. There a "man" came to Jacob, whom he took to be the Angel of the Lord. Jacob wrestled with the man all night in one last, desperate attempt to gain God's blessing through his own power. In the end, the man touched Jacob's thigh, forcing his hip out of joint. At last Jacob was broken, physically as well as spiritually. When morning dawned, the long night of struggle with God was finally over. "And as [Jacob] passed over Penuel the sun rose upon him, and he halted upon his thigh" (Genesis 32:31). Though Jacob was physically weaker, he was spiritually stronger. He was finally willing to trust God's ways rather than his own strength.

BROKEN AT THE POINT OF STRENGTH

The sinews of the thigh are among the strongest parts of the human body. God didn't break Jacob at his point of weakness but at his point of greatest strength. Until Jacob was convinced that he could not reach God's destination on his own ability, he could never receive the blessing. By breaking Jacob at his point of strength, God showed him the need to trust His ways.

God will likely do the same for you. Your greatest obstacle to spiritual growth and effective ministry is not your biggest weakness but your most prominent strength. If you are called to preach, you will likely rely first on your personality, speaking ability, and the craft of persuasion to reach people. To fulfill God's purpose for your life, you must come to rely on His anointing alone. Human skill is valuable, but not when it becomes an impediment to the leading of the Spirit. If you are called to be a leader, you may be tempted to resort to manipulating people, information, or finances in order to get others to follow your vision. And that may seem right because, after all, you're doing God's work. But you will never be effective in doing God's work through man's ways. Even in a place of simpler service, you will be tempted to rely on your own hard work, long hours of sacrifice, or your intellectual ability to get the job done. You must be broken of the idea that you have within you all it takes to serve God and succeed. You must be willing to trust God to do His work in His way.

After wrestling with God, Jacob walked with a limp. Yet he was dancing in spirit as he discovered the true path to God's blessing—trust. I imagine God dancing with joy over Jacob, who had finally surrendered his strength, skill, and cunning to rely wholly on the Father.

Perhaps you are living with a limp, a spiritual or emotional hurt, because you wrestled with God and lost. Reframe that picture of yourself into a child dancing with his or her father. We must relearn the lesson that serving Jesus Christ is not a matter of doing a lot of hard things. It is comes down to doing simple things with a fresh anointing. That may be the hardest lesson of all. God is calling us to relearn the basics. Something about our complex society leads us to believe that our success, even in ministry, is all up to us. It isn't. Achieving God's goals is a matter of trusting God in the ways that He leads us.

Several years ago, when our son Lee, was about six years old, I was deep in prayer and feeling some despair after struggling to reach a higher level of effectiveness in my ministry. Lee came into the room and, seemingly out of nowhere, said, "Daddy, you are trying too hard." God used the words of a child to deepen my understanding of the spiritual life. It isn't how hard we try that makes us effective in the kingdom. It is how simply and completely we are willing to trust the ways of God.

If you are like Jacob, trying to follow God's path for your life but really taking your own journey, make the decision to surrender. Give up on trying to do it all and have all the answers. Recognize that the God who calls you is faithful, and you can trust His methods as well as His intentions. Make the decision to trust God's ways.

Yet we must harbor no illusions about the ease with which we will arrive at our goal. Every worthwhile objective, including an intimate relationship with the Father, requires a heavy dose of a very unwelcome virtue. To find out what it is, we must make a trip to the most inhospitable place on the face of the earth. We begin the next chapter aboard a sailing ship headed for Antarctica.

YOUR NEXT MOVE

Your next move is to commit yourself to doing things in God's way by surrendering control of your life to Him. To do that, sincerely follow these steps.

1. Spend an extended time in prayer (one hour or even a full day) asking God this: "Show me the areas of my life that are not fully surrendered to you."

2. Ask the Holy Ghost to fill your heart completely, cleansing any areas of hidden sin or stubborn disobedience that you have discovered. Open yourself to the Spirit's work.

3. Enlist an accountability partner (or invite your small group) to help you walk in obedience. Give them permission to question or challenge you on the points of self will that you have surrendered to God.

LESSON 4
Stick with it

On December 29, 1913, the following advertisement is said to have appeared in The Times newspaper: "Men wanted for hazardous journey. Small wages, bitter cold, long months of complete darkness, constant danger, safe return doubtful. Honour and recognition in case of success."[4] The ad was supposedly placed by Sir Ernest Shackleton who led The Imperial Trans-Antarctic Expedition, 1914–17, also known as the Endurance Expedition after the ship in which Shackleton sailed. Shackleton set forth from Plymouth, England, on August 6, 1914, but by November, the height of the Antarctic spring, Endurance became icebound in the Weddell Sea before ever reaching Antarctica. For many months ship and crew drifted along with the ice pack, Shackleton and his men effectively prisoners of the ice. By October 1915, the changing conditions of the next Antarctic

---

4. Though this part of Shackleton's story has been widely reported, no copy of such an ad can be found; therefore, the veracity of this story cannot be proven.

spring brought such pressure upon the hull of Endurance that it began to crack. On November 21, the crew was forced to abandon ship.[5]

With Endurance sinking below the ice, Shackleton and five others began the heroic voyage that truly lived up to the name Endurance. After spending several weeks on the ice pack at a floating station they dubbed Patience Camp, Shackleton and his men piled into three lifeboats and threaded their way through the ice to Elephant Island, where they found a place to put ashore. From there, Shackleton and five others set sail in one of the boats, bound for the whaling settlement on South Georgia island—some eight hundred miles to the northeast. The voyage would require navigating this trackless expanse against adverse winds and with pinpoint accuracy. From the start, the twenty-two-foot open boat was beset by heavy seas, drenching both men and supplies with icy water. Several days into the voyage, a northwesterly gale, described by Shackleton as the worst he'd seen in twenty-six years at sea, nearly destroyed the craft. After fourteen grueling days at sea, the crew was drenched, cold, and exhausted. Two days later, they dragged themselves to shore at South Georgia's King Haakon Bay, only to discover that they were on the opposite side of the island from the whaling station. Having come this far by sea, they now faced a grueling trek overland.

Shackleton and his men rested for five days and made plans for a trek across the rugged island terrain. Having driven screws salvaged from the lifeboat through their boot soles for added traction, they then began their march across the icy mountains without the aid of a map. At the close of that first day, needing to descend to the valley below them before nightfall, they risked

---

5. Details of Shackleton's adventure are reported in Sir Ernest Shackleton, C.V.O., *South: The Story of Shackleton's Last Expedition 1914–1917* (New York: The MacMillan Company, 1920).

everything by sliding down a mountainside on a makeshift rope sledge. There was no question of rest—they travelled on by moonlight, moving upwards toward a gap in the next mountainous ridge. Early next morning, they sighted Husvik Harbour and realized they had chosen the right path. At seven o'clock they heard the steam whistle sound from Stromness, "the first sound created by an outside human agency" that any of them had heard since December 1914. After a difficult descent, which involved passage down through a freezing waterfall, they at last reached safety after marching for thirty-six hours straight.

On January 10, 1917, a revived Shackleton returned to Elephant Island aboard the Aurora to rescue the seven surviving members of the original party. Though Shackleton never made it back to the Antarctic, the goals of his expedition were finally achieved some forty years later when the Commonwealth Trans-Antarctic Expedition, 1955–58, successfully made the first land crossing of the continent.

The aptly named Endurance Expedition provides a vital insight into the spiritual journey that you are about to take and reveals the fourth prerequisite for your success. You can be certain that your journey will take longer, be more difficult, and call for more sacrifice than you now expect. You will need a great deal of patience and endurance for this trek to God's purpose. To develop a lifelong, growing, intimate relationship with God, you must learn to persevere.

FROM DISASTER TO DESTINY

Accepting your place in God's family means moving from disaster to destiny; however, this will require both endurance and patience. Endurance is the determination that says, "I'm going to continue following God's purpose in God's way even though it's not turning out as I'd envisioned." Patience is the inner calm that enables you to say, "I can wait for God to reveal His plan in His time." When you follow God's purpose for your life and commit to trust God's way—His leading, timing, and methods—you will need plenty of patience and endurance.

For one thing, God seldom moves according to our timetable. You may find that God is taking you by a different, slower route to your purpose than you would have chosen. You may have thought you would be more successful by now or in a different place of service than where you find yourself. You may even be in what seems to you like the wrong place. Yet if you are pursuing God's purpose in God's way, you're right on schedule and right where you need to be. This calls for patience and endurance. Let's remember a few things about persevering in God's will.

First, perseverance requires a joyful attitude. It is impossible to endure with a sour spirit or to be patient with a bad attitude. If you are going to endure and be patient, it has to be with a spirit of joy. Joyfully, we can give thanks to the Father who qualifies us to share in the inheritance of the saints in the kingdom of light, even when our immediate circumstances aren't to our liking. " For he has rescued us from the dominion of darkness and brought us into the kingdom of the Son he loves" (Colossians 1:13 NIV).

Second, you can never see the whole picture, but God can. God never takes someone out of a place unless He has another place prepared. What seems like a difficult time in your life—even a disaster—is not destruction. It is simply a transition from one place to another, from one glory to another, and from one level of faith to another.

Third, your attitude can help or hinder your ability to persevere. By your own words, you can either talk yourself out of being patient or build your endurance. The choice is up to you. Talking down to yourself and saying, "the blood does not work" or "God must have forgotten me" can bind God's hands and keep Him from working. Remember that you have been redeemed, you have been forgiven, and your heavenly Father delights in you. When you talk as if your God-given purpose will never be fulfilled, it won't be. You won't take delight in following God, and He cannot dance over you. When you accept His love as surely as you have accepted His water baptism or the infilling of His Spirit, your words will reflect that positive reality—even when you feel discouraged.

Fourth, to endure, you must keep faith in God and His promise. It is possible to build a religion around what God has not done. Many people do this every day. They are envious of the miracles they have seen in others' lives, or of the favor of God working in the ministries of others. As a result, the focus of their relationship with God is on what He has not done for them. By doing that, they limit what God can and will do in them and through them. God does not work in the absence of faith! On the other hand, we free the Spirit to move when we accept and trust God's Word. His blessing comes through His promises, not through your circumstances. Keep your focus on the truth. Keep faith in the Word of God and in His call upon your life. There will come a time when God is ready to move in your life. You will miss that moment if you lose faith in God's Word.

Fifth, remember that you are qualified to receive God's blessings. As one of God's children, Jesus Christ has made you worthy to enjoy a harvest, to experience revival, and to come into your anointing. These blessings are not reserved for a select few; they are for the whole body of Christ. Sometimes the reason we don't make the spiritual progress we'd like to make is that we feel we are somehow not qualified to receive it. Yet God is calling His church to expect and anticipate His best in this last hour. God is calling dreamers. We cannot achieve those dreams on our own, but when we engage God in our lives, all things are possible. While we do have a defilement of sin that we cannot remove, have inherited a debt we cannot repay, and suffer from a dire deficiency that we cannot eliminate, we have been rescued by God in His mercy. Paul admonished the Colossians to lift up their heads, square their shoulders, and walk with a backbone as straight as a saw log rather than listening to the voice of the devil saying, "You do not deserve God's blessing. It does not belong to you." Anything God has promised this church, He has qualified you to receive. Believe, and receive it. Live right, walk in the light, and watch God operate by the power of His might. Remind yourself, "I've got purpose and potential," for you surely do.

ACCEPT YOUR ANOINTING

As an example of perseverance in the face of difficult times, let's consider King David. According to some scholars, David received three anointings in his life. But further study reveals a fourth anointing. The first anointing was when Samuel anointed David king over Israel. Samuel spoke David's prophetic future into existence. That anointing set David on the path to God's purpose and released him into his destiny. David's second anointing came when the men of Judah anointed David king. At this point David had received only a portion of the inheritance given him by Samuel's anointing. He was king over just two of the twelve tribes, Judah and Benjamin. Even so, David was willing to praise God, believing the entire promise would be fulfilled. We can do that as well; celebrate what God has done—even if the work is yet unfinished. We can rest in what we have received because we know that God has more planned for us.

David's third anointing came when all Israel came to Hebron and anointed David king, giving him power to advance the kingdom. According to Isaiah 9:6–7, we are promised a never-ending increase in the kingdom of God and of His peace. From these verses we learn that the government has to be on His shoulders before we will see the increase. This simply means that He must be the one making decisions. One reason we don't receive the increase we expect is that we do not want God's dominion over our lives. We must accept God's authority along with His anointing.

David received a fourth anointing, and it came after he was stricken with disaster. David committed adultery with Bathsheba and murdered her husband, Uriah. God's judgment on David resulted in their infant son being stricken with illness. David was completely distraught, pleading with God for the child's life and fasting for seven days. When the boy died, however, the Scriptures say that David got up and "anointed himself." In the wake of disaster, one brought on by David's own failure, he was able to go on and reclaim his anointing.

If you are to persevere in following God's purpose in God's way, you must learn to anoint yourself. You must call to mind every promise the Lord has given you, every prophetic word ever spoken over you. During the long days of hard work and the agonizing nights of weariness and fear, you may come to the place where you doubt God is even there, let alone in control of your destiny. This is the time you must anoint yourself, remembering everything that a Samuel in your life has said to you and every way the Lord has blessed you. Get your journal or diary out and recall the many times God has delivered you. Pick up your Bible and read the great promises that God has given us. If there is no kind voice to be found around you, go to a private place and anoint yourself with oil. Reclaim the promised future that God has already given to you.

Perhaps you have had the experience of seeking to borrow money and being told that you needed a cosigner. A cosigner has credit that you don't. When that person puts his name on your papers, you can walk away with whatever you like. When you were baptized in the name of the Lord Jesus Christ for the remission of sins (Acts 2:38), Jesus placed His name on your papers. You are working from His credit now, not your own. You have His promise that "whatsoever ye shall ask in my name, that will [He] do, that the Father may be glorified in the Son" (John 14:13). You can't do this in pride and arrogance or though your own ability. You can do it only by the grace of the One who has the authority to qualify you.

The devil can't shut you down or shut you out of what God has prepared for you. "Eye hath not seen, nor ear heard, neither have entered into the heart of man, the things which God hath prepared for them that love him. But God hath revealed them unto us by his Spirit" (1 Corinthians 2:9–10). God is preparing you for your destiny by removing the defilements of sin, poor attitudes, and incorrect perspectives that have hindered your progress. That may take time and will be difficult. Yet the Bible is clear: All who have been forgiven are qualified for their inheritance. When you begin to experience the growth in grace, the maturity, and the effectiveness that God has planned for you, that is the moment the Father will dance.

Do you trust the God who loves you? Do you have a right concept of God, as a loving heavenly Father who delights in you?

Have you chosen God's direction for your life? Are you committed to remaining close to Him, refusing to be distracted or to drift from the goal of an intimate relationship with Him?

Are you willing to trust God's ways? Will you wait for God's timing, trust His decisions, accept His will, and let go of the idea that you can gain spiritual goals through your own vision, ability, and hard work?

And are you willing to persevere? Have you accepted that this is a lifelong journey, not a quick trip to the convenience store? Are you fully committed to the lifelong endeavor of knowing God and finding your delight in Him?

Congratulations! You are ready to begin the adventure of your life. You are ready for the big dance—the dance of delight with your heavenly Father.

YOUR NEXT MOVE

Your next move is to steel yourself through the Spirit to face the challenges to growth that lie ahead of you. To do that, choose one or more of the following activities.

1. Write your answer to this question: "What circumstance now causes you to doubt God or tempts you to abandon faith?" Enlist a friend to pray with you for strength to continue your journey.

2. Draw a timeline of your life, a horizontal line on a piece of paper with your birth date on one end and today's date on the other. Place an X on the line for each major challenge you have faced in life. Place a V (for "victory") on the line to mark each time God has intervened in your life or carried you through a crisis. Thank God for His steadfast presence during times of trial.

3. Sometimes the best way to be encouraged is to encourage others. Name a person you know who is facing a serious challenge, and contact that person to affirm and pray with them.

PART 2
The Dance of Delight

STEP 1
Seek a Relationship with the Father
The Principle of Divine Relationships

They were married on February 10, and the chilly London weather matched her attitude toward matrimony. She was an independent twenty year old with money and a career, a rarity in her day. Strong willed and forward thinking, she had no desire to be yoked for life to a man, let alone one she barely knew. When advised that marriage would be the best way to escape the control of her domineering mother, the outspoken young woman called it a "shocking alternative."[6] Yet in the staid culture of nineteenth-century England, even a wealthy woman had little autonomy, and marriage seemed the best option. She reluctantly agreed to entertain a suitor. Surprisingly, they hit it off, and he proposed marriage on their second meeting. She accepted. Mutual respect turned to friendship, then to affection, then to one of the great romances of the modern age. On her wedding night, Queen Victoria wrote in her diary about her husband, Prince Al-

---

6. Christopher Hibbert, *Queen Victoria: A Personal History* (Cambridge, Mass.: Da Capo Press, 2000), 104–105.

bert, "His excessive love & affection gave me feelings of heavenly love & happiness I never could have hoped to have had before!... His beauty, his sweetness & gentleness—really how can I ever be thankful enough to have such a Husband!"[7] This beloved husband and best friend stood at Victoria's side for twenty-one years as she ruled the largest empire the world has ever seen. Then he died.

Victoria was devastated by the loss. She wore black for the remainder of her life, more than forty years. She became reclusive, seldom venturing to London but preferring her secluded residences at Windsor Castle, Osborne House, and especially Balmoral, the private estate in Scotland she and Albert had acquired together. The independent, vivacious young woman had become the widow queen, a symbol of grief.

John Brown was seven years younger than Victoria, and in every way different. She was royalty; he was a servant. She was well-bred and dignified, a true lady. He was a rough outdoorsman, a ghillie as the Scots say, or wilderness guide, at Balmoral. Despite her grief over the loss of Albert, or perhaps because of it, Queen Victoria and John Brown formed an unlikely friendship. She came to depend on his competence and companionship. Brown devoted himself to his queen, carrying her over muddy highland paths and fending off potential assassins. They became inseparable. Insiders referred to Brown as "the queen's stallion." Victoria, sovereign of a kingdom on which the sun never set, called Brown her dearest friend.[8] Upon Brown's death, Victoria commissioned a life-size statue of the rugged Scot, to be installed on the grounds of Balmoral, which stands today. The inscription

---

7. Ibid., 123.
8. Julia Baird, "*A Queen's Forbidden Love,*" NYTimes.com, August 29, 2014, http://www.nytimes.com/2014/09/01/opinion/a-queens-forbidden-love.html.

reads: Friend more than Servant. Loyal. Truthful. Brave. Self less than Duty, even to the Grave.

Over the years, many have speculated about the decorum of the relationship between Victoria and her improbable companion, though no conclusive evidence of impropriety exists. What we do know from this story is a simple idea that is written into the fabric of human existence: even a queen needs a friend. Though separated from nearly everyone by her position, power, and wealth, Queen Victoria longed for the simple comfort of companionship. We are made for relationships.

That shouldn't be surprising, because we are created by a relational God. The first step in developing intimacy with God is to discover that He wants a relationship with you and to pursue that relationship with passion. To move from the peaks and valleys of sporadic spirituality to the constancy of daily communion with God, you must develop a daily relationship with Him.

GOD IS RELATIONAL

Many people are surprised to speak of God, who created the universe and stands so far above it, as a person, yet it is entirely appropriate to do so. He is a living being who relates to others. Thinking of God as a person doesn't make Him more like us. Just the opposite! To call human beings persons refers to the fact that we are made in God's image, for God is a relational being. God is love (1 John 4:8), and He constantly seeks to know and love us. God the Father loves you so much that He came to earth as Jesus Christ, to bring you back into a relationship with Him. This is the pattern for all proper relationships: loving, serving, self-giving. And remember that you and I are created in the image of God

(Genesis 1:27). That means we are relational too. We are created to hunger for relationships with one another and a relationship with God. So the hunger you feel for a connection with your heavenly Father is something He feels too. He wants to be close to you! God created you to have a relationship with Him.

RELATIONSHIPS IN ACTION

What does it mean that God enters into relationships with people? Let's see that in action as we review the lives of some of the major figures in the Bible. In each case, we'll learn something about what it means to have a relationship with God.

ABRAHAM: RELATIONSHIPS REQUIRE TRUST

We know Abraham as the father of the faithful and a friend of God. This is where we begin our journey into the life that God wants to give us—in forming a friendship. Abraham was one of the first people with whom God formed a relationship, and we can learn a lot from the way Abraham related to God.

Two people cannot be in a relationship unless there is some commonality between them. The prophet Amos asks, "Can two walk together, except they be agreed?" (Amos 3:3). Abraham walked in agreement with God. Abraham trusted God. That faith was strong enough to withstand many challenges. Abraham's faith was strong enough for him to leave his homeland and follow God, and through years of waiting for God's promises to be fulfilled. Abraham trusted God to such a degree that God actually formed a covenant—a formal agreement—with him. You can read the details in Genesis 15.

Your daily devotion to God, trusting Him, speaking with Him, relying on His help and guidance, will bring you deeper into a relationship with Him. God commanded the people of Israel to listen to the Bible read every seven years, and the king was to read the law every year. By spending time in God's Word, you will enter into greater agreement with Him. You will learn to trust God more, and your relationship will grow.

ISAAC: RELATIONSHIPS REQUIRE SACRIFICE

Isaac is the "middle child" of the Patriarchs' family tree—Abraham, Isaac, and Jacob. His story is easy to overlook. Yet Isaac was the child of God's promise, born to Abraham and Sarah in their old age. And his story teaches us something vital about having a relationship with God: relationships require sacrifice.

You may know the story of the sacrifice of Isaac on Mount Moriah (see Genesis 22). When we read this story, we are usually most impressed by Abraham's willingness to sacrifice his son. Let's not overlook Isaac's role here. He was old enough to be aware of what was happening, and the fact that he asked his father, "Where is the lamb for the burnt offering" (Genesis 22:7) seems to indicate that he was not merely aware, but a willing participant. Isaac trusted God enough to be the sacrifice!

At some point in every relationship, you will be called upon to sacrifice for the other person. That's really the essence of a friendship isn't it? It certainly is the backbone of a good marriage. Each person must be willing to put the other first. Your relationship with God is no different. Are you willing to give up your time to spend it with God? Are you willing to spend time in worship, hearing from God and fellowshipping with others? What alterations are you willing to make to your lifestyle in order to draw closer to God? A relationship always involves giving.

JACOB: RELATIONSHIPS ARE FUELED BY PASSION

The story of Jacob reveals the necessity of passion in your relationship with God. Even though Jacob had many failures and faults, they did not disqualify him from having a covenant relationship with his God. That's because Jacob had a lifelong passion to know God and to have God's blessing on his life. As we saw in an earlier chapter, Jacob at first pursued that blessing in the wrong way, using his own cunning, strength, and skill. He had to be broken by God before he could enter fully into a relationship with God. But when he learned to trust God, Jacob's passion led him to enjoy the blessing of God.

What is your level of passion in your relationship with God? How much do you want God's presence in your life? Are you willing to push through obstacles and persevere in order to receive God's blessing? No relationship can be successful when it is one sided. You must be a partner with God in your relationship with Him. God dances over people who ardently seek to know Him as Father.

MOSES: RELATIONSHIPS DEMAND COMMITMENT

When Moses asked God what His name is, the Lord responded, "I AM THAT I AM" (Exodus 3:14). That statement alone conveys a lesson about the relational nature of God. He does have a name—or at least is willing to be known by one. Though scholars puzzle over the exact meaning of that name, it is clear that God does indeed want us to know who He is, and that He is unique. God is who He is, which is who He has always been. He is personal, eternal, and unchanging.

There's more to this story, however. God followed up on His answer to Moses by giving more information. The Bible introduces this second statement about God's name with the word moreover. In this case, that really means something more like "better yet" or "more importantly." So when God told Moses His name, He added a statement that we might paraphrase like this: "But even more important, tell the children of Israel that the LORD God of your fathers, the God of Abraham, the God of Isaac, and the God of Jacob, has sent me: that is my name forever" (Exodus 3:15). In essence, God told Moses that He would rather be known as the God of those with whom He had a relationship. Those three men built a relationship with God so special that God was not at all hesitant to be named as their God. God commits Himself to His people, and He expects His people to commit themselves to Him as well.

A covenant relationship involves commitment. In fact, at the time Moses asked about God's name, God was commissioning Moses to return to Egypt and free the Hebrew people from slavery. Why? So they could go into the wilderness and worship Him (see verse 18). God extended the covenant He made with Abraham to all of his descendants. The Bible tells us that God wants everyone to enter into a relationship with Him (see 2 Peter 3:9).

Establishing daily trust in God (walking in agreement with God, as Abraham did) requires sacrifice, passion, and commitment. Every major character in both the Old and New Testaments who has been used by God has displayed these attributes, and they are most clearly seen in the life of Jesus Christ, the supreme role model for all Christian behavior. And Jesus added at least one more aspect to what it means to have a relationship with God: intimacy.

JESUS: RELATIONSHIPS LEAD TO INTIMACY

Those who are in a relationship become close over time. Jesus invites us into a family relationship with Himself, teaching us that we have the privilege of calling God our Father (Matthew 6:9). We all are given the privilege of calling God by the term Abba, similar to our word Daddy. This is a term of endearment. Think of it! We have permission to approach God on a level of intimacy never before dreamed possible. God wants to be close to His people. He wants to be known by the people with whom He fellowships.

This was foreign to the ancient Middle Eastern view of God and sometimes to our view as well. The people of Jesus' day simply could not look up to heaven and describe God as Daddy. In all the lists of names associated with God and their elaborate descriptions of His attributes, none referred to God as Abba. To do so removes the formality and ritual from our relationship. It destroys the need for liturgy and opens the door for true fellowship. When that occurs an amazing thing happens: a person cries out to a powerful Father who cares.

A disappointing experience with an earthly father can cloud your perception of your heavenly Father. You may not be able to relate because of that past hurt. Perhaps you have no reference point on earth from which to compare this delighted and delightful heavenly Father. If you have trouble relating to God as your Father because of painful family relationships and memories, know that the Messiah whom Isaiah calls "The everlasting Father" (Isaiah 9:6) will never fail you. He is nothing like the earthly father who may have disappointed and hurt you so badly. God is a loving, gentle father who craves an intimate relationship with you.

How intimate is your relationship with God? Does He feel like a true Father to you? Do you have a sense of security as His child? You can develop this sense of closeness with the Lord by spending time with Him in prayer, solitude, reflection, and by sharing your joys and sorrows with Him, just as you would with your closest friend. God desires an intimate relationship with each of His children. He wants to be close to you.

HOW TO SEEK A RELATIONSHIP WITH GOD

Most people wonder how to develop a relationship with God. It is one thing to know that God is a being, a person to whom you can relate. It is something else to actually develop this relationship with someone whom you cannot see and who speaks to you often through indirect means such as Scripture and the guidance of the Spirit. We have already learned that a relationship with God depends on trust, requires sacrifice, is fueled by passion, demands commitment, and leads to intimacy, but how does that work in real life? What do you do to pursue this relationship with God?

Interestingly, people seldom have a question about how to develop a relationship with any other person. Most of us have been doing it since we were children, and it comes quite naturally. We understand that to develop a friendship, you must first meet someone, then spend time with that person, sharing information about yourself, learning about the other person, and doing things together. Those activities provide the context in which a friendship can grow.

The same is true of developing a relationship with God. It needs a context in which to grow. The following suggestions for developing your relationship with God may seem very much like the things you do in developing human relationships. Just remember that your goal is to develop a daily delight in the presence of God in your life—a relationship that is free from the spiritual highs and lows you may have experienced in the past. Usually, a relationship begins when someone is willing to break the ice and make an introduction. It is no different in your relationship with God, so that is where we begin.

MEET GOD THROUGH FAITH IN JESUS

This is your first step in developing a relationship with God. If you have not already done so, get "introduced" to God by faith in Jesus Christ. Jesus said, "I am the way, the truth, and the life: no man cometh unto the Father, but by me" (John 14:6). That amazing statement reminds us that the only way we can know God is through Jesus Christ. The only true way to God is to know His true name, which is Jesus. In fact Jesus said, "He that hath seen me hath seen the Father" (John 14:9).

Have you come to know Jesus Christ? Have you placed your faith in Him? If you have not begun your relationship with God, the place to start is by acknowledging that Jesus Christ is the One True God, our everlasting Father. Put your trust in Jesus today. You can do that with the simplest of prayers, something like this: "Lord Jesus, I know that I don't deserve to have a relationship with God, but I truly want that. I'm so sorry for being selfish and ignoring God for so long. I trust you, Jesus. Please show me the way. Amen."

COMMUNICATE CONSTANTLY

Relationships are developed by spending time together. You may believe it's impossible to spend time with a person that you never see, but that's not at all the case. Time spent in communication is perhaps the most valuable of all, as my friends Larry and Heather could tell you. They met while attending a conference in Florida, and they formed an immediate connection and were sure they wanted get to know one another better. The only problem was that they lived over a thousand miles apart. In the days before video chat was available, how could they possibly create a relationship, and explore the possibility of a romance, when they couldn't even see each other? The two began by exchanging emails and phone calls. They talked constantly, racking up over 3,000 minutes of call time in a single month, and wrote hundreds of emails, talking about everything from their childhood memories to their hopes for the future. "I feel like the distance actually helped," Heather said. "There was no small talk. We immediately started sharing things that matter with one another."

"We talked about anything and everything," Larry agrees. "We became close friends very quickly." And they became more than friends. When Larry proposed marriage after knowing her for only four months, she said yes immediately. Their happy marriage is a testament to the fact that you can get to know someone you can't see. To develop a relationship with God, you must learn to spend time with Him—though in different ways than you might be used to.

Daily Conversations. Daily conversation with God through prayer is the most basic way to spend time with Him, to communicate what is on your mind, and to listen for His response in times of silence, reflection, and through the ministry of the Holy Ghost. The Spirit is really the medium of your communication with the Father. For the apostle Paul tells us that "the Spirit itself beareth witness with our spirit, that we are the children of God" (Romans 8:16). So it is through this daily communion with God, through the Spirit, that we have confidence in our new relationship. And when we are at a loss for words, the Spirit is our helper. "Likewise the Spirit also helpeth our infirmities: for we know not what we should pray for as we ought: but the Spirit itself maketh intercession for us with groanings which cannot be uttered" (Romans 8:26).

Communication is the lifeblood of any relationship, and your daily conversations with God will deepen your sense of God's presence and become a welcome part of your day. How do you develop a prayer life? The same way you develop any other relationship—by doing it consistently.

Weekly Gatherings. If you're like me, you probably enjoy getting together with friends and family to share a meal or just get caught up on life. That's why we love Sunday dinners, holidays, birthday parties, and even things like a softball league. Being with a group of friends strengthens your relationships with each of them—and with the group itself.

That same dynamic comes into play in pursuing a relationship with your heavenly Father. It's great to be alone together each day for conversation, but it's also good to gather with a group of likeminded friends to worship the Lord together. When you are faithful in attending church, you'll find that something interesting happens. Your love for God and for others will grow. This will happen gradually. There may be no mountaintop moment or "breakthrough." Yet over time, your attachment to God, your faith in Him, your knowledge of Him, and your love for His people will increase dramatically. As Jesus reminds us, He Himself is present in any gathering of believers (Matthew 18:20). The writer of Hebrews put it this way: "And let us consider one another to provoke unto love and to good works: Not forsaking the assembling of ourselves together, as the manner of some is; but exhorting one another: and so much the more, as ye see the day approaching" (Hebrews 10:24–25). Going to church is one of the best ways to further your relationship with God, and with His other children!

"Letter" Writing. My friends Larry and Heather found that writing to each other, even in this electronic age, was a great way to develop a relationship. The same can be true in your relationship with the Father. That's one reason God communicated with us in writing through the books of the Holy Bible. These inspired writings contain history, poetry, letters, laws, advice, and even love songs. As you spend time reading God's Word, the Holy Spirit will open your mind to know God better. Jesus said of the Holy Ghost, "When he, the Spirit of truth, is come, he will guide you into all truth" (John 16:13). What a wonderful designation for God's Spirit—the Spirit of truth. Part of the Spirit's role is to help you understand God's Word. As you read, He will open your mind to the truth. You will understand God better, know Him more fully, and your relationship will grow.

A second way that you can deepen your relationship with God through writing is by doing the writing yourself. As the familiar saying goes, "Thoughts disentangle themselves when passing over lips and through pencil tips." In other words, when you speak or write your thoughts, you come to understand them better yourself. In conversation, we sometimes call this talking it out. Another way of "talking out" your thoughts is by keeping a journal. Journaling is a bit like writing a prayer, though perhaps not so formal. It is simply thinking on paper, airing your thoughts and exploring your feelings in the presence of God. You may choose to address your thoughts to God, but you don't have to be quite that formal. As you write your experiences, your hopes and dreams, and your fears and failures, the Spirit will speak God's words to your mind. You may find that you know both yourself and God much better as a result of keeping a journal.

DO THINGS TOGETHER

To develop a friendship with someone, you generally find some activity to do together. Believe it or not, the same holds true in your relationship with the Father. This isn't going for a hike together or taking up a hobby. The thing you do together with God is His mission in the world. When you share your faith, feed the hungry, clothe and house the homeless, it is as if you are doing these things for Jesus Himself (see Matthew 25:31–46). The Father takes great joy in seeing His children carry on His work in the world. When you serve others in the name of the Lord, He not only empowers you for the work through the Holy Spirit but also accompanies you on the journey. Just as His disciples were not immediately aware that Jesus walked along with them on the road to Emmaus (see Luke 24:13–35), you will find that God is with you as you go about His business in the world. As you work together, your relationship will deepen.

SEEK CONSTANT CONTACT

As your relationship with God grows, you will eventually come to a place where you are constantly in contact with the Father. The great spiritual master Brother Lawrence referred to this as "the practice of the presence of God." Whether you are in the kitchen cooking, driving to work, sitting in a business meeting, or changing diapers, you have the sense that God is right there with you. This is what the apostle Paul spoke of when he said to "Rejoice evermore. Pray without ceasing. In every thing give thanks: for this is the will of God in Christ Jesus concerning you" (1 Thessalonians 5:16–18). No matter where you are or what is happening, you know that God is there with you. You take delight in Him, and you know that He takes delight in you. All of your thoughts are more or less directed to God. You are enjoying the dance of delight as your Father dances with joy over you.

LORD OF THE DANCE

I have been preaching since I was eleven years old, and through the years I have seen many expressions of joy and dancing under the inspiration of the Holy Ghost. I have seen brothers and sisters so moved in the Spirit that they would sing, shout, and dance before the Lord. How thrilling to see those who are touched by the Spirit enter into that joy. Yet I cannot help but wonder if our Father has often been weeping while we have been shouting. Is it possible He is saddened because He longs to find those who will go beyond a momentary experience of His presence and live in a daily, constant relationship with Him? If our experience with God were the best indicator, would we say that God still longs for someone to share His heart on a daily basis? Are we good examples of what it means to walk so closely with God that He would dance with delight over us?

I hope we will be such examples. May we never think of God as our divine errand boy, someone who submits to our whims and fancies, who is at our beck and call but is easily forgotten. Let us enter into a deep, abiding, intimate relationship with the God who loves us so much that He would dance with delight at the very thought of us. This is God's great desire, as Sydney Carter reminds us in song, "Lord of the Dance."

I danced in the morning when the world was begun
And I danced in the moon and the stars, and the sun
And I came down from heaven and I danced on the earth
At Bethlehem I had my birth

I danced for the scribe and the Pharisee
But they would not dance and they wouldn't follow me
I danced for the fishermen, for James and John
They came with me and the dance went on

I danced on the Sabbath and I cured the lame
The holy people said it was a shame
They whipped and they stripped and they hung me on high
And they left me there on a cross to die

I danced on a Friday when the sky turned black
It's hard to dance with the devil on your back
They buried my body and they thought I'd gone
But I am the dance and I still go on

They cut me down and I leap up high
I am the life that'll never die
I'll live in you if you'll live in me
I am the Lord of Dance, said he

Dance, then wherever you may be
I am the Lord of the Dance, said he
And I'll lead you all, wherever you may be
And I'll lead you all in the dance, said he
Dance, said he[9]

---

9. Sydney B. Carter, "Lord of the Dance" (Carol Stream, Ill.: Hope Publishing Company, 1963). Used by permission. License Number: 78220

The Lord of the Dance wants a relationship with you. God wants this relationship so much that He was willing to pay the great price of dying on the cross for us. Will you join Him in this Dance of Delight?

YOUR NEXT MOVE

Your next move is to enter a relationship with God, or to strengthen the relationship you have. To do that, choose the following activity that fits your situation.

1. Enter a relationship with God by repenting of your sins, being baptized in the wonderful Name of Jesus for the remission of sins and receive the Gift of the Holy Ghost evidenced by speaking with tongues. There is no substitute for being truly born again into God's family, and you can do this today.

2. Write the following elements of relationship on a sheet of paper: trust, sacrifice, passion, commitment, intimacy. Beside each one, give a brief description of (a) the current state of this aspect of your relationship with God, and (b) what you will do to enhance that area of your relationship. Share the results with a friend, accountability partner, or small group.

3. Establish the daily spiritual discipline of prayer. Identify a daily time of prayer, and pray daily for the next thirty days. Ask a friend to keep your accountable for this practice.

STEP 2
Praying without Ceasing
The Principle of Kingdom Prayer

In the ancient world, these creatures were revered, even worshiped. Some actually believed they had supernatural powers. The Greeks, for example, thought this unusual being could direct lost travelers toward their destination. The Egyptian *Book of the Dead* lists them as minor gods who guided souls of the departed through the underworld. Other civilizations called them *necromancer* or *soothsayer*. The Khoi people of southern Africa revered this tiny animal to such a degree that it became known in Afrikaans as *Hottentotsgot*, or god of the Khoi.[10] What is this mysterious, powerful, spiritual being? None other than the praying mantis.

Mantis religiosa, as it is properly known, is not really beseeching the almighty. This odd insect, of which there are more than 2,400 species, is a predator, not a pray-er. Most mantises are am-

---
10. Fredrick R Prete, Harrington Wells, Patrick H. Wells, and Lawrence W. Hurd, eds., *The Praying Mantids* (Baltimore, Md.: The Johns Hopkins University Press, 1999), 4–5.

bush predators, meaning that they lie in wait for their prey. They hold their raptorial forelegs in a retracted position, ready to spring upon an unsuspecting fellow bug. This makes mantises appear to be clasping their hands as if in prayer. Do not be deceived. These stick-like creatures are incredibly powerful—and ravenous. Larger mantises sometimes eat smaller members of their own species, and they are capable of devouring lizards, frogs, and even small birds. Those "praying hands" are lightning fast, able to strike in one twentieth of a second, and incredibly strong, capable of lifting objects 800 times the mantis's own weight. Before being too hard on our predecessors in the ancient world, we should acknowledge that they did stumble onto a vital spiritual principle: there is an unmistakable connection between power and prayer.

KINGDOM PRAYER

God delights when His children pray. And God is calling His people to prayer, but not just any kind of prayer. God delights most when His children pray in accordance with His will and in complete faith. God delights in kingdom prayers. We must do more in our prayers than just repeat, "Jesus, Jesus" or "O God, O God." Our vain repetition doesn't impress God, and it doesn't scare the devil. However, we know that "the effectual fervent prayer of a righteous man availeth much" (James 5:16). And Jesus said, "whatsoever ye shall ask in my name, that will I do, that the Father may be glorified in the Son" (John 14:13). Earnest, fervent prayer in the name of Jesus brings great power to bear on your own life and circumstances. Kingdom prayer mobilizes heaven and puts the devil to flight.

What is kingdom prayer? It is the prayer that Jesus taught us to pray: "Thy kingdom come, Thy will be done in earth, as it is in heaven" (Matthew 6:10). Kingdom prayer is prayer focused on God and His kingdom, in agreement with His will, and prayed with boldness and faith. This is the kind of prayer that delights the Father.

KINGDOM PRAYERS ARE SELFLESS

T. W. Barnes taught me something very powerful when he said, "Brian, I have seen men die before their time because they tried to use their gift on themselves. Your gift wasn't given to you for yourself but for others. The only way to walk in divine health and victory is to walk with Jesus in joy, peace, and righteousness." Another great preacher, Johnny James, put it this way: "We are saved to serve." Praying for one's own needs is good, and praying to get out of trouble is certainly encouraged, but kingdom prayer is far better. This is one of the greatest spiritual disciplines you can develop because it is prayer that puts you squarely in agreement with God and His purposes. This is much more effective and powerful than simply praying for blessings upon yourself.

Here is another way to understand this concept. People who truly seek God's blessing must give Him permission to say no as well as yes to their requests. To pray only for ourselves is to continually ask for God's yes. To pray for the kingdom, you must be equally ready and willing to accept God's no. I have lived long enough to rejoice in the opportunities that came my way but which God refused to let me accept. He closed one door only to open a better one later on. I thank God for those closed doors. If you are not so fully submitted to God in your spirit that you cannot let Him close doors, then you will never be able to find the true will of God for your life. Kingdom praying says, "Not my will but thine be done." It asks God for His kingdom to come and His will to be done on earth as it is heaven.

Jesus' prayer in the garden of Gethsemane provides our best example of kingdom prayer. Calvary loomed as a great shadow over the heart of Jesus as He made His way to Gethsemane with His disciples. As the pressure of the moment began to swell in His spirit, the pain was almost unbearable. It was at this moment that Jesus chose three disciples to travel farther into the olive grove, hoping they would share in the excruciating trial of His decision to allow Himself to be crucified. Instead they slept, unaware that their eternal destiny was being determined just a few feet away. So Jesus continued alone.

In Gethsemane, two choices were set before Jesus; two roads stretched out into the future. Which would He choose? This was more than a matter of choosing the easiest or most convenient way for Himself. The Father's will was at stake. Jesus knew that making the harder choice would bring countless souls to salvation. The easier choice would be to save only Himself. Although Jesus was born to die on the cross and knew very well that was His purpose, the decision was still a struggle. There at Gethsemane He submitted His will completely to the Father and consciously determined to carry out His mission to the bitter end. In the garden, He was able to pray the ultimate kingdom prayer, "Not my will, but thine, be done" (Luke 22:42).

The mockers at the cross said, "He saved others, himself he cannot save" (Matthew 27:42). They spoke the truth, but from a scorner's point of view. Jesus could have chosen to save Himself. But if He had, there would be no church, no Pentecost, and no hope for humanity's redemption. Jesus' great kingdom prayer surrendered His life to gain ours. He put the Father's will, the kingdom, you and me, ahead of Himself. That is kingdom praying.

Historians agree that the Battle of Gettysburg, fought in July 1863, was the decisive battle of the Civil War. Of course, there were other major battles both before and after Gettysburg, and nearly two years passed before Robert E. Lee's Army of Northern Virginia surrendered at Appomattox Court House. Yet the great battle fought on the hills outside that sleepy Pennsylvania town marked the decisive turn in the war. Gethsemane was that for Jesus. It was the decisive moment in the great spiritual war for the souls of humankind. Jesus prayed a kingdom prayer before that battle, and the victory was assured. The great devotional writer Oswald Chambers wrote, "Prayer is *the* battle."[11] He may have been thinking of Gethsemane.

To pray kingdom prayers, you must surrender your will so completely to the Father that you are able to pray in complete agreement with Him, "Thy will be done." This is the kind of prayer that delights the Father. Yes, the Father delights in giving good gifts to those who ask Him, and there is nothing wrong with that. Yet His greater desire is that His children should seek first His kingdom and His righteousness (Matthew 6:33). When you begin to pray in this way, you will find greater joy in your journey. You will know that the Father dances over you with delight. Kingdom prayers are those that are focused on the Father, His will, and His kingdom, not on ourselves.

---

11. Oswald Chambers, *My Utmost for His Highest: An Updated Edition in Today's Language*, ed. James Reimann (Grand Rapids, Mich.: Discovery House Publishers, 1992), entry for October 17.

KINGDOM PRAYERS ARE BOLD

Alfred Lord Tennyson observed, "More things are wrought by prayer / Than this world dreams of."[12] The story of Daniel proves that to be true. This biblical hero shows us another aspect of kingdom prayers: they are bold prayers, and they require boldness to pray them. Daniel's conflict in prayer proves you can change the destiny of a nation through kingdom prayer. Daniel was a fixed star as he battled against a powerful empire, and he won the war. His secret to victory can be found in six words: "He kneeled . . . as he did aforetime" (Daniel 6:10). Daniel prayed three times a day, every day, regardless of the fact that a law had been passed against it. Daniel was a kingdom prayer. His prayers were not for himself but for others, and nothing could compel him to stop. The tyrant king could not force him to bow to his golden image. The jealous courtiers could not keep him from the appointed hour for prayer.

Ezekiel points to Daniel as one of the great intercessors of Old Testament times (see Ezekiel 14:14). It was Daniel's praying which broke the chains of the Babylonian captivity, setting Israel free to fulfill her divine purpose. Daniel's visible enemies tried to keep him from the act of prayer. His invisible adversaries opposed the answering of his prayer, as Daniel later learned: "The prince of the kingdom of Persia withstood me one and twenty days" (Daniel 10:13). Daniel understood what Paul later wrote to the early Christians, that "we wrestle not against flesh and blood, but against principalities, against powers, against the rulers of the darkness of this world, against spiritual wickedness in high places" (Ephesians 6:12). Once, the angel Gabriel came to Daniel while he was praying (Daniel 9:21). Michael, the "chief of princes," became an ally with Daniel against his unseen foe (Daniel 10:13,

---

12. Alfred Lord Tennyson, "Morte D'Arthur," *Poems of Alfred Lord Tennyson 1830–1865*, new ed. (London: Oxford University Press, 1910), 110.

20). Invisible forces rule the world, but they are defeated through prayer. As Daniel shows us, even the course of global events can be influenced by the persistent praying of one man.

Kingdom prayer is bold prayer. It asks for God's will to be done on earth, just as in heaven. This kind of prayer is not achieved in a single session nor even through a single episode, as when Daniel risked his life by defying the king's command against prayer. It took seventy years of faithful intercession before Daniel witnessed the emancipation of his people. Are you committed to a lifetime of kingdom praying? Are you willing to pray day in and day out, regardless of immediate results? Will you trust that your prayers are powerful and effective, even when you do not personally see the results? Will you have the faith to keep praying when others mock or ridicule you? Will you have the faith to make a "big ask" of God, knowing that when you pray in faith and in agreement with God's will, nothing is impossible?

Kingdom prayer is a consistent, unflinching, unyielding prayer in agreement with God's will. It overflows with confidence in God. It is directly in line with His vision for the world, and it is the most powerful kind of prayer you can imagine. Are you willing to move beyond petitioning God only for your own needs and only when it feels urgent or convenient to do so? Are you willing to enter into a life that is characterized by daily, faith-filled, bold prayer for the will of God? This is the kind of prayer that makes your Father dance with delight.

KINGDOM PRAYERS ARE POWERFUL

The Judean date palm was a staple of the ancient near east for centuries. Prized for its sweet fruit and cool shade, this tree was one of the most common plants during Bible times. In fact, Tamar the daughter-in-law of Judah, and Tamar the daughter of King David both appear to have been named after this lovely palm.

Though the Judean date palm was still flourishing at the time of Christ, by AD 500 it had completely disappeared. It remained extinct for some fifteen centuries until archeologists, excavating the palace of Herod the Great in the early 1960s, discovered a cache of seeds stowed in a clay jar. The seeds were known to be some 2,000 years old. These ancient spores were stored in a drawer at Bar-Ilan University in Tel Aviv for over forty years. Then in 2005, a botanical researcher named Elaine Solowey decided to plant one. She was less than optimistic about the prospect. "I assumed the food in the seed would be no good after all that time. How could it be?" she said. But the seed was good, and it did sprout, producing the first Judean date palm to be seen in over 1,500 years. Today, this wonder plant continues to thrive and has even produced flowers, signaling that it may be able to reproduce itself.[13]

A seed may be small—and even old—yet every seed contains power. It contains the power to become. Jesus compared the kingdom to a tiny seed, the mustard seed. "Which indeed is the least of all seeds: but when it is grown, it is the greatest among herbs, and becometh a tree, so that the birds of the air come and lodge in the branches thereof" (Matthew 13:32). And Jesus said, "But as many as received him, to them gave he power to *become* the sons of God, even to them that believe on his name" (John 1:12, emphasis added). You have the power to become a child of God. God's children, collectively as the church, have tremendous potential in the world. Kingdom prayer releases that creative power. Kingdom prayer pursues with passion the spiritual possibilities

---

13. John Roach, "2,000-Year-Old Seed Sprouts, Sapling is Thriving," National Geographic Society, November 22, 2005, http://news.nationalgeographic.com/news/051122-old-plant-seed-food/.

of God's promises. Kingdom prayer is like the seed of the Judean date palm. It contains within it the power to become. Though others may believe that you or the church have no power left, your kingdom prayer enables you to become all that God wants you to be.

Kingdom prayers envision possibility. Kingdom prayers call upon God to enable you, your church, your community, even the world, to become what He wants you to be. Who prays such prayers? The Hall of Faith in Hebrews 11 lists many kingdom prayers. In most cases, we don't know the precise words they prayed, but we do see the results. Think of men and women like Abraham, Moses, Rahab, Gideon, and so many others "who through faith subdued kingdoms, wrought righteousness, obtained promises, stopped the mouths of lions" (Hebrews 11:33). These people were able to see *what could be* and pray accordingly. Those kingdom prayers were answered in mighty ways.

Are you willing to allow God to develop the seed of new life in you by continually praying prayers of possibility—kingdom prayers? Can you envision what God might do in your life in response to faith? What about your family? Your church? Your community? Remember the biblical heroes of Hebrews 11. Nothing is impossible with God.

KINGDOM PRAYERS REQUIRE FAITH

Kingdom prayer is not easy because it involves sacrifice and risk on our part. Yet this is the kind of prayer that delights the Father, and it's the kind of prayer each of us should aspire to pray. To pray kingdom prayers, you must have the firm faith that comes from a close, daily connection with God. Let's take a look at an example of some children of God who lost that anchor, and we will see how disastrous the result can be.

Before the Israelites entered the Promised Land, they sent twelve spies to make a survey of their new home, Canaan. Why send spies if God had already promised to give the land to the Israelites? Did they really need strategic military data to conquer the land? Of course not. God directed every campaign. They had no need to gather this information. They should have been able to walk in confidently and let God handle all the details.

When God gives us a gift, He also gives us the chance to be involved with Him and to be a partner in His work. God allows for our passionate pursuit of His promises, and that is exactly what each of us should long for. This is exactly where kingdom prayer comes in. We have the privilege of investing ourselves in God's work, seeing what may become of our efforts together, and praying that this great plan of God's should be accomplished here and now. That's kingdom prayer in a nutshell.

Ten of the spies, however, lost their anchor—their trust in God. They got so wrapped up in the details of conquering the land that they began to look at the problem as if it were theirs alone to solve. In short, they took God out of the equation and never put Him back in it. The original question they had been assigned to answer—how to conquer the land—soon became an entirely different question: Should we even try? By leaving God out of the equation, they turned all the positive signs into negatives ones. Consequently, their conclusion was, "That's impossible!" They rejected their original mission.

Without a firm connection to the Father—relying on Him for strength, seeking His will, trusting Him—no kingdom prayer is possible. That disconnection brings something far worse than the loss of a good possibility. It brings destruction. Let's review how that played out with the twelve spies.

First, they lost confidence in what God's salvation had done—and could do—in their lives. This is evident from the spies' report: "We were like grasshoppers in our eyes, and so we were in their eyes" (Numbers 13:33). Convinced they had no chance of success, the spies saw themselves as insignificant, virtually giving up in the face of the enemy.

Second, the spies made excuses for their lack of power and courage. They actually indicted Moses for taking them out of Egypt! (Numbers 14:2). To avoid blaming themselves for their lack of faith and obedience, they made excuses. Someone else had to be blamed.

Third, the spies woke up and realized the opportunity they had squandered. Unable to bear the great disappointment and failure, they heroically declared: "Now let's enter the land" (Numbers 14:40). They desperately wanted to recapture the lost opportunity, but Moses informed them that it was too late. The opportunity was gone, and any attempt to enter the land contrary to God's decree was certain to end in tragedy.

Fourth is the final and most painful step in the process of self-destruction. The spies could not bear living with failure for the rest of their lives, so they entered the land contrary to God's command, only to be slaughtered by their enemies (Numbers 14:45).

This is the alternative to a kingdom mind-set, which is evidenced by kingdom prayer: self-destruction. When we fail to trust God completely, remaining anchored in His Word, connected to Him through daily prayer, we will follow a similar pathway to defeat. To stop the process of self-destruction there is something we must immediately do: reconnect with God.

Each of us has a vision for our lives, an idea of what we expect to do and what difference we believe we can make in the world around us. The Bible teaches that when our vision grows from our connection with God, our ability to achieve that vision will transcend all boundaries. Since God can do anything, success depends only on His will and our obedience to it. Without that connection, our ability is only as great as our own ability—which is to say, very limited indeed. When we are connected closely to the Father, we are able to do great things. Jesus said, "Abide in me, and I in you. As the branch cannot bear fruit of itself, except it abide in the vine; no more can ye, except ye abide in me. . . . If ye abide in me, and my words abide in you, ye shall ask what ye will, and it shall be done unto you (John 15:4, 7). In other words, when we remain connected with the Father through faith in His Son, we can pray kingdom prayers.

How close is your connection with the Father? Kingdom prayers cannot be pulled out of a hat like a rabbit, made to appear whenever wanted. They rise from a heart that is joined with the Father's through meditation on the Word, and of course, consistent daily time spent in prayer. We seek the Father's will, surrender to it, and envision the possibilities that may come. We cannot know what private thoughts went through the minds of the two faithful spies, Joshua and Caleb, as Caleb announced to all the world, "Let us go up at once, and possess it; for we are well able to overcome it" (Numbers 13:30). What we do know is that their experience confirms the power of faith. When we dare to dream the impossible and pursue God's best with great passion, we will receive it.

PRAYING KINGDOM PRAYERS

Kingdom prayers are selfless because they put God and His kingdom first. They are bold because they are undertaken consistently, continually, regardless of opposition or outcome. They are powerful because they tap into God's creative vision for the future. And they require a deep connection with the Father in order to be effective. Kingdom prayer is exactly what the church needs today, and it is the thing that will move your own spiritual life forward. If prayer birthed the first Pentecostal experience, then prayer can create another such revival for us. Therefore, the priority of the twenty-first-century church must be to pray selfless, bold, powerful kingdom prayers. Only then can we receive the power needed to evangelize our world.

That all sounds wonderful, but if you have tried to pray big, bold, selfless prayers then you know how challenging it can be. We may have a desire to delight the Father, to move the kingdom forward, to unleash the tremendous potential of the church, yet we feel defeated in prayer. We do not pray effectively—we do not pray kingdom prayers—because we don't know how or give up too quickly.

We have already seen that Jesus provides our perfect example of kingdom praying through His experience at Gethsemane. Let's explore that experience a little more deeply to find some clues about how to pray in a way that delights the Father.

MAKE PRAYER A PRIORITY

The first step in praying kingdom prayers is to make them a priority. You must realize the tremendous value of such prayers, for I can assure you that the devil does! We notice from Jesus' experience at Gethsemane that the devil knew exactly where Jesus was. John 18:2 says, "And Judas also, which betrayed him, knew the place: for Jesus ofttimes resorted thither with his disciples." The one who betrayed Jesus knew exactly where He prayed. Satan knows the place where you pray and whether or not you pray at all. His first strategy is to keep you from prayer by keeping you from your place of prayer—whether a literal place or a mental place that leads you to seek the Father. If Satan can discourage you from even attempting prayer, his battle is won.

Immediately after Jesus' baptism, right after a voice from heaven declared that Jesus was the son of God, Jesus was led by the Spirit into the wilderness to fast and then be tempted. Satan's first words were, "If thou be the Son of God." Hell hears what heaven says about you, and the devil will challenge everything God wants to do in your life. Nevertheless, we achieve victory if we are willing to pay the price in kingdom prayer. Prayer is more than saying words over and over again with a loud voice. We need real communion with God through focused, kingdom praying. We need to settle the issue of our will and find out what we really need from God. God allows Satan to know the place of our praying, challenging our faith to focus on what we really need. Prayer is communion with God, and it is also a battlefield. Realize how vital your prayer life is, and pray!

WITHDRAW TO PRAY

Let's return to Jesus' experience at Gethsemane. We read in Luke 22:41: "And he was withdrawn from them about a stone's cast, and kneeled down, and prayed." Jesus withdrew from the others a short distance to pray. This was not the first time Jesus withdrew from others in order to pray. In fact, He made a habit of it. Luke tells us that Jesus often withdrew to be alone in prayer (5:16). In order to pray effectively, you must withdraw from others. Prayer in groups is a wonderful experience. Do not neglect your prayer meeting or small group prayer time, and of course the prayers of the church in corporate worship. Yet there is a type of prayer that you can do only when you are alone with God. To pray kingdom prayers, you must develop the habit of a personal, private prayer time.

When you do, get ready for criticism. The word, withdraw in a certain context means "to unsheathe the sword." When you get alone with God, it is like drawing your sword from its scabbard and preparing yourself for battle. When you start praying for God's kingdom to come and not your kingdom, you are going to place yourself where stones can hit you. Remember that Jesus Himself experienced this. Mark tells us when Jesus slipped away by Himself to pray, people started looking for Him, seemingly a little annoyed that He had gone off by Himself (see Mark 1:35–37). You may be criticized for being aloof, or for the actions you take based on what you learn of the Father's will through prayer. When you pray kingdom payers, it can distance you from others, even other Christians.

Yet we must get alone with God to discover His will and submit ourselves to it. The measure of our anointing is not how we pray in the public sanctuary but how we spend our time alone with God. That is where we discover what He wants from us and how we can please the Father.

MOVE FORWARD IN PRAYER

Mark's gospel describes Jesus' prayer at Gethsemane this way: "And he went forward a little, and fell on the ground, and prayed that, if it were possible, the hour might pass from him" (Mark 14:35). It is interesting that Mark does not simply say Jesus went away from the others, but that He went forward. Kingdom prayers always move forward. They do not seek to regain the past or even maintain the status quo. Kingdom prayers move us forward into the future God envisions for us.

How would you characterize your prayers in that regard? Are you praying to get back to what you once had? Are your prayers focused on what was, what is, or what will be? Yesterday's blessing is over. As thrilling as God's work was in days gone by, He wants to do a new thing, a better thing in your life, your family, and your church in the future. Kingdom prayers lead us forward to receive what we have never had before. Our prayer must discover the will of God for our lives and then become a commitment to fulfill it. This is so much more than simply asking God to bring back the good old days.

Moses provides a great illustration of this principle. When Pharaoh pursued the Israelites toward the Red Sea, they were terrified and cried out to God. They were stuck, and they knew it. But they were looking only backward, at the Egyptian army. That's when God spoke to Moses and said, "Wherefore criest thou unto me? Speak unto the children of Israel, that they go forward" (Exodus 14:15). Kingdom prayers are forward focused, and they result in forward action.

Too often we pray only to feel better on the inside, not waiting to receive the specific word from God needed to fulfill His purpose. We pray as a kind of placebo. We don't think it will do much, but at least it will make us forget our problems for awhile. To pray kingdom prayers, you must have a forward focus. Pray believing that your heavenly Father delights to hear your prayers, and that He has a hope and a future for you.

GO FARTHER IN PRAYER

Jesus taught a great lesson in prayer when He told the story of the persistent widow. Luke begins the story by telling its purpose: the story is to show us that we should always pray and not give up (Luke 18:1). Jesus Himself modeled that principle at Gethsemane. Matthew tells us that "he went a little farther, and fell on his face, and prayed, saying, O my Father, if it be possible, let this cup pass from me: nevertheless not as I will, but as thou wilt" (26:39). The Gospel writers use different terms to describe this same event. Luke tells us that Jesus withdrew to pray; Mark says that He went forward; and Matthew pictures Jesus going farther. Matthew emphasizes that idea by mentioning that Jesus prayed the same prayer three times. Jesus didn't give up easily! We might say that He went farther, and farther, and farther in prayer. He did not stop until He had reached the point not only of seeing the Father's will but also of surrendering to it. Jesus prayed through to victory.

Sometimes we just do not go far enough in prayer. We stop when we should go on. Kingdom prayer is not a perfunctory exercise, like some of the prayers we offer before meals or at bedtime. Some of those prayers are not prayers at all, mere rituals that we do by habit. Prayer must be a habit, but it must be something more. Kingdom prayers are prayers made in earnest. They are prayers that do battle. They are prayers that seek resolution. To pray kingdom prayers is to pray and not give up.

What about your prayers? Do you go the extra mile in prayer to clearly see God's will? Do you pray through to the point of surrender? Do you experience victory through your prayers? Or do you stop short, praying only enough to say that you've "taken it to the Lord"? Satan may know your place of prayer, and what keeps you from it. You may have to pay a price with others to be alone with God. But if through prayer you will move forward and at some special moments of trial, go farther still, you will experience the kind of prayer that delights the Father. In those moments, it is His good pleasure to give us the kingdom. What a destiny!

DANCE OF THE HAND

I am convinced that much more is possible for each of us—and for all of God's church—than we currently realize. Too often, we more closely resemble the ten faithless spies than the two who were able to see the possibilities. No doubt, kingdom prayers require a great deal of faith and sacrifice. Yet they are the key to unlocking the possibilities that God has for our lives and for our world.

Often, God does not work in the midst of our chaotic lives because we tie His hands through our lack of faith—and the prayerlessness that results from it. Our unbelief keeps Him from doing what He might do, just as the unbelief of Jesus' hometown neighbors prevented Him from doing miracles there (see Mark 6:1–6). Only when we release God's hand can we expect Him to deliver us.

We can restrict God's works in our lives through false assumptions about how God works. In our arrogance, we think we have all the answers. As long as your hand—meaning your will and actions—occupies God's space, His hand is not free to work.

We long to see the manifestation of God's presence. We want to see His power manifested in our lives and in our circumstances. Interestingly, our word manifest is derived from a Latin root meaning dance of the hand. When we release God's hand into our life, He can reorder the chaos into something beneficial. Our kingdom prayers become a kind of dance of the hand in which we surrender our "hand" (or will and actions) to God's hand so that He can freely move in our lives. Have you done the dance of the hand with your heavenly Father? Is His power manifested in your life? Commit yourself to praying big, bold, powerful, selfless prayers, the kind that take great faith and constant connection to the Father. Then you will see your heavenly Father dance with delight over you.

YOUR NEXT MOVE

Your next move is to strengthen your prayer life by consistently praying bold, sacrificial, powerful prayers. To do that, try this ninety-day discipline of prayer.

1. Enlist at least two prayer partners who will journey with you into kingdom prayer. Agree to meet at least weekly for prayer and accountability.

2. Discuss your prayer concerns together, sharpening each other to be bolder, more faith-filled, and less self-focused in your prayers. Pray together over the concerns you identify, then pray daily on your own over those same requests.

3. Review your prayer list and God's response each week. Make a visible reminder of God's actions, such as placing a stone in a jar for each answer to prayer or writing the results on a whiteboard.

STEP 3
Remain Constant
The Principle of Divine Consistency

The team had a checkered history. It began in Seattle, but after only a year and a half the franchise was reassigned to Baltimore. By the mid-1980s, the team had claimed yet another city as its adopted home. The club had also bounced from league to league, starting with the old All American Football Conference in 1946. It later joined the National Football League, and was subsequently shuffled off to the NFL's American Conference. Even the team's colors were changed somewhere along the line, from silver and green to blue and white. Sure, there had been some good seasons, including a Super Bowl win in the early '70s. But those days were long gone.

After a long string of personnel changes, losing seasons, and seemingly endless heartbreak for the fans, the Colts finally won a division championship in Indianapolis in 1996. Hopes were high in the Circle City but were quickly dashed as a dropped pass on the last play of the conference championship game foiled the dream of a Super Bowl appearance. During the next season, the Hoosier Dome saw as many fans sporting the colors of the Chicago Bears or Cincinnati Bengals as the blue and white of the hapless Colts. This team, it seemed, couldn't get anything right—at least not for long. Indianapolis was becoming better known by its other nickname—Naptown, the city where nothing happens.

By 1997, everyone from the sports writers to the players to the fans was tired of the up-and-down performance. It was time for a change, and a big one; anything to bring consistency to this haphazard excuse for a football club. That change came with the death of longtime Colts owner, Robert Irsay. With his passing, control of the team shifted to his son, Jim Irsay, just thirty-six years old at the time. The younger Irsay promptly fired the general manager and brought in a wily football veteran named Bill Polian to manage the club. At the next year's NFL draft, Polian faced a golden opportunity to bring stability to the lackluster team, for he held the number one draft pick, and with it the possibility of choosing the very best college football player of the year. At last, the Colts might move beyond the inconsistent performances of the past with a true franchise player, a player strong and solid enough to build a team around.

The choice was obvious to everyone. Ryan Leaf was the standout college quarterback of the 1997 season. The twenty-one-year-old from Washington State had already compiled impressive stats, completing 317 passes for an astounding 3,666 yards. In his senior season, Leaf led his team to the Rose Bowl, was voted a first team All American, was named Pac-10 Offensive Player of the Year, won the Sammy Baugh Award given each year to the nation's top collegiate quarterback, and was a finalist for college football's most coveted honor, the Heisman Trophy. Best of all, the kid had an arm like a rocket launcher. This had to be the simplest decision ever presented to an NFL general manager: draft Ryan Leaf and put your team on the road to victory.

The choice was obvious to everyone except Bill Polian. The veteran of many NFL drafts and a shrewd judge of talent saw something in Leaf that troubled him. For one thing, Leaf's official prospect profile, while noting that he had an incredibly powerful arm, went on to say that he "can be very inconsistent throwing the ball and misses too many open receivers." The report added that he was "overly emotional and has to be in the middle of everything." Perhaps worst of all, the scouts noted that Leaf was "self-confident to the point where some people view him as being arrogant and almost obnoxious."[14] As if to prove the point, Ryan Leaf was a no-show for his interview with the Indianapolis Colts.

Another college quarterback did keep his appointment with Bill Polian: Peyton Manning from the University of Tennessee. He too was a highly rated prospect of the class of 1998. He too was a first team All American, and winner of numerous athletic awards and honors. Yet Manning had something more. He excelled academically. He was a member of the Phi Beta Kappa Society and earned the National Football Foundation's National Scholar-Athlete Award. Though not as explosive on the field, he seemed more mature—safer. So against the advice of his field scouts, Bill Polian chose stability over uncertainty. With the first pick of the first round of the 1998 NFL draft, Polian selected Peyton Manning.

Manning went on to play in four Super Bowls, winning two. He is the first and only quarterback to amass 200 career wins, five NFL MVP awards, and fourteen Pro Bowl selections. He passed

---
14. "Ryan Leaf, QB," ESPN Sports Zone, archived copy captured December 7, 1998 by Web.Archive.Org, https://web.archive.org/web/19981207060713/http://nfldraft98-espn.sportszone.com/html/player/player17.html.

for over 4,000 yards in fourteen seasons, an NFL record, and he is the league's all-time leader in both passing yards and touchdown passes. His steady, commanding on-field presence earned him the nickname "The Sheriff." Manning also founded a charity that assists underprivileged children and underwrote the founding of a children's hospital in Indianapolis.

Ryan Leaf played for three teams during his disappointing four-year stint in the NFL, and his post-football life has been marked by legal troubles. Bill Polian knew that when it comes to winning at sports, steady performance counts far more than razzle-dazzle. The player who can overcome the highs and lows, the emotions and intrigues, and perform consistently is the one who will win.

THE PRINCIPLE OF DIVINE CONSISTENCY

"I am the LORD, I change not," God declared through the prophet Malachi (3:6). This foundational statement of God's character gives us the principle of divine consistency, which we see echoed in the New Testament: "Jesus Christ the same yesterday, and to day, and for ever" (Hebrews 13:8). Simply put, God is always the same. He is reliable, dependable, unchanging. In His character and in His actions, God is consistent.

Our problem is that we are not consistent. We are fallible, prone to experience highs and lows, peaks and valleys. Like a streaky quarterback, we may be on top of our game one week and slump the next. Because our emotions are inconsistent, we have an experience of God that is inconsistent too. When we have a burst of faith and good feelings, we believe we can conquer the world for God—and we may try. A day later, we may be discouraged, believing that God has abandoned us when the only thing that has changed is our feelings. God is just as capable, just as loving, and just as powerful today as He was yesterday and will be tomorrow. It is we who must discover how to regulate our lives so that we have a consistent spiritual experience.

God is always delighted when His children call out to Him. Yet I can't help but think that He is weary of our spiritual ups and downs, which closely match our mood, emotions, or circumstances. How He must long for us to walk calmly and deliberately with Him, not swayed by the vagaries of emotion, excitement, or passing sentiments. God wants us to have a consistent walk with Him, a consistent and reliable experience of His presence, grace, and power. God is constant, and He desires that we be constant as well.

How do we achieve that? Each of us faces ups and downs in life; and our emotions, however changeable, are real. They affect our ability to think and relate to others and to keep faith. How do we develop a consistent spirituality amid the many changes we face in life? To answer that question, we will examine this principle of divine consistency using two images. The first is air, and the second is rock. As we explore these two metaphors for your spiritual life, you will see how to move beyond the ups and downs that have plagued you in the past and develop a consistent experience of God.

CREATING YOUR OWN ATMOSPHERE

Let's begin with the metaphor of air. The atmosphere is mostly invisible to the human eye, but it is all around us. We live in it, and we live by it. We must take air into our lungs in order to breathe. The atmosphere—and what it brings—can quickly impact our lives. If you have ever been in a smoke-filled room or driven past a field where a farmer was working, you know how rapidly particles of smoke or dust can clog your airway, producing discomfort. Before long, you can't see and can barely breathe. Pollution, wind, or precipitation can dramatically affect your life, even your health and safety.

Your emotions are like that as well. They are like the air in which you live and breathe. You may be largely unaware of them, at least initially, yet they color the way you see the world. When your emotions are positive, you feel that you can tackle just about anything. Yet anger, disappointment, frustration, sorrow—any negative emotion can derail your mind and heart. Your emotions are your atmosphere. They surround you wherever you go and influence how you encounter the world around you. When they are sunny, you thrive. But when your emotions turn cloudy it can ruin your day—or worse.

What if you could create your own atmosphere? What if you had a filter that could remove all pollutants, moderate the force of the wind, and turn all precipitation into big, fluffy clouds so that every day was warn and sunny? Well, you'd certainly have a more predictable and enjoyable life. And what if you had a way to filter your emotions so that the positive ones didn't cause you to go to extremes and the negative ones didn't derail your faith and relationships? In other words, what if you could mitigate the effect of your emotions on your spiritual life?

The good news is that you can do exactly that. You can create your own atmosphere, so to speak, by taking control of your attitude and your reactions. Emotional ups and downs are a significant struggle for many people so I don't say this lightly, but you can find balance in your emotional life. You can have a consistent walk with God—and with others as well.

Let's find out more about that by exploring the lives of some well-known, and some lesser-known, characters from the Bible. We begin with one of the great men of the Bible, but one whose name you may never have heard. Let's meet Benaiah.

BENAIAH: ON YOUR WORST DAY, TRUST GOD TO BE AT HIS BEST

Nestled in the list of David's mighty men in 1 Chronicles 11, we discover an amazing individual who teaches us a lesson in constancy. Here we learn the basic truth that God's overcoming victory in our lives is not a pie-in-the-sky wish, and it does not depend on our emotions or circumstances. It is based on the consistency of God.

When listing David's mighty men, the writer of Scripture gave us a bit of detail about each one. We see three exploits of a man named Benaiah, and each one teaches us a lesson about divine consistency.

> *Benaiah the son of Jehoiada, the son of a valiant man of Kabzeel, who had done many acts; he slew two lionlike men of Moab: also he went down and slew a lion in a pit in a snowy day.*
>
> *And he slew an Egyptian, a man of great stature, five cubits high; and in the Egyptian's hand was a spear like a weaver's beam; and he went down to him with a staff, and plucked the spear out of the Egyptian's hand, and slew him with his own spear. (1 Chronicles 11:22–23)*

Benaiah was used to taking on long odds. He defeated two "lionlike" men of Moab, proving that he had the courage to fight when outnumbered. He also defeated a more heavily armed and larger opponent, proving that he was willing to fight when out gunned, so to speak. And when he stepped into a pit to do battle with a lion on a snowy day, Benaiah took on the longest odds of all. It was a winter day, with the cold and snow affecting everything about the fight—his muscle condition, reflexes, visibility, footing. And the fight was in a pit, a place from which he could not escape. This was a do-or-die context. Yet Benaiah didn't flinch. He was willing to trust God for victory even in the face of a terrifying foe and under the worst possible conditions. By doing so, he demonstrated a firm belief that God will always be at His best, even when conditions are the worst.

Certainly you are facing, or will face, a terrifying challenge under the worst possible conditions. You may receive news about your health or that of a loved one's that frightens you. You may be facing a monumental challenge in your work or in your ministry. Perhaps your challenge is at home, in your marriage, finances, or family. And you are not at your best. You are frightened, angry, overwhelmed, perhaps discouraged. Here is the good news. God will still be at His best, even on the worst day of your life. Applying the principle of divine consistency means matching your mood to God's strength, not your circumstances.

It was a cold, snowy day when Benaiah did battle with the lion. Yet he made his own weather. His constant faith in God brought heat and comfort, and he was able to tackle an overwhelming challenge. You can too. Trust God to be at His best, even when you are at your worst.

ELIJAH: PUT GOD'S PURPOSE FIRST

Elijah was another biblical weatherman. He too created his own atmosphere when he faced down four hundred fifty prophets of Baal on Mt. Carmel (see 1 Kings 18). He stood on the windswept mountaintop as it was kissed by the last rays of the setting sun. Before him stood a sacrifice of two bulls, prepared on an altar of stone. The challenge was to call down fire from heaven to consume the sacrifice. The prophets of Baal had tried and failed; now it was Elijah's turn. Like Benaiah, Elijah had no way out. He would prove God's faithfulness or die in the attempt.

Here is where the story gets interesting. He first repaired the altar of the Lord, which had been broken down. Then he drenched the altar, sacrifice, wood, and all, with four large jars of water. And then he did it again. And again. Then he looked up to a cloudless sapphire sky, and prayed a big, bold kingdom prayer: "LORD God of Abraham, Isaac, and of Israel, let it be known this day that thou art God in Israel, and that I am thy servant, and that I have done all these things at thy word. Hear me, O LORD, hear me, that this people may know that thou art the Lord God, and that thou hast turned their heart back again" (1 Kings 18:36–37). In an instant, fire fell from heaven and consumed the sacrifice—wood, stones, dust, water, and all.

Notice that before he attempted to call God into action, Elijah unified himself with divine purpose. He was careful to repair the altar that was broken down, for he knew that unity was necessary for God to act. If you feel as if you are disconnected or at variance with God's purpose, there is only one remedy; you must repair the altar in your life. Elijah used water on his sacrifice to make sure the heathens knew this was no trick. In essence, he declared, "I will douse all of man's fire in order to receive God's fire." You can try to make your own fire—that is, to make God's work happen in your way and your time—but that never works. You need a complete change of atmosphere. You must filter out the little bits of self-interest, self-protection, and self-pity that cloud your relationship with the Father. Purify the air by seeking first His kingdom and His righteousness. Nothing then will be impossible for you.

Elijah won his victory on the mountaintop, but what about the valley? Let's turn to the best-known Bible story, and the best one to demonstrate that God gives victory in the valley—David in the Valley of Elah.

DAVID: BANISH FEAR WITH CHILDLIKE TRUST

Like Elijah, David faced an impossible enemy. Just a stripling, a lad, he faced the mighty giant Goliath. The entire army of Israel was cowering in fear, unwilling to face the Philistines or their champion, Goliath. As a mere boy visiting his brothers at the front, David was disgusted both by the giant's foul taunts and by the Israelites' unwillingness to stand up for the Lord. You know the rest of the story. Armed with nothing but a sling, he chose five smooth stones from the brook, then shouted to the enemy:

> *Thou comest to me with a sword, and with a spear, and with a shield: but I come to thee in the name of the* L<small>ORD</small> *of hosts, the God of the armies of Israel, whom thou hast defied.*
>
> *This day will the* L<small>ORD</small> *deliver thee into mine hand; and I will smite thee, and take thine head from thee; and I will give the carcases of the host of the Philistines this day unto the fowls of the air, and to the wild beasts of the earth; that all the earth may know that there is a God in Israel.*
>
> *And all this assembly shall know that the* L<small>ORD</small> *saveth not with sword and spear: for the*

battle is the Lord's, *and he will give you into our hands. (1 Samuel 17:45-47)*

David entered the valley outnumbered, overshadowed by a towering foe, and with a cowering army at his back. Yet he prevailed against Goliath because he would not allow fear to pollute his faith. He was outraged that anyone would insult the name of the Lord, and he never doubted for a moment that God would back his move, giving victory with a slingshot, a rock, a stick, or even his bare hands if it came to that. David knew that the real power in his life came not from his own skill or strength but from the Lord.

David's naïve trust in God is exactly the filter you need to win victory in the valley. Jesus said, "Except ye be converted, and become as little children, ye shall not enter into the kingdom of heaven" (Matthew 18:3). When you can trust God in the way a child trusts his mother to care for him, or a boy will leap into the air trusting his father to catch him, you will have victory in the valley. Looking at the long odds, the dark shadows, the overwhelming circumstances you face only breeds fear. Childlike trust filters out fear, creating an oxygen-rich atmosphere for your faith.

AN UNNAMED WOMAN: SEEK GOD WHEN YOU NEED HIM MOST

Let's move to the New Testament to learn a lesson in creating an atmosphere of constancy from a woman who is completely unknown—that is, unnamed. When a woman with the issue of blood touched the hem of Jesus' garment, she was immediately healed (see Mark 5:25–34). This unnamed woman had suffered for years, consulted every doctor available, and spent everything she had, yet grew only worse. She was out of options and out of hope. If anyone ever had a right to self-pity, this woman did. No one could blame her for living in a cloud of despair.

Yet she made the decision to reach out to Jesus. She was timid about it, for sure. Far from asking to meet Jesus, this woman didn't even want to be noticed. Yet she had faith enough to believe that even touching Jesus' garment would bring healing. Her faith needed no priming or prepping to make it work. Her belief in God's goodness and Jesus' power was constant and consistent. All that was needed was the right connection.

God is consistent regardless of your emotional condition. We mistakenly believe that God is somehow more real or more available when we feel better about ourselves. God is the same all the time. We think God is more likely to be at work in a worship service when we enter into it with a proper attitude, but the truth is that God is always present with His people and always ready to display His power. If we could be more like this anonymous woman whose faith has become known around the world, we would be just as ready—or even more ready—to experience God when our emotions are down.

Create your own atmosphere by seeking God when you need Him the most. Don't hang back from prayer or worship when you feel down. That's the very time you need them! Don't allow your frustration, anger, or sadness to keep you from reaching out to the very One who can help you. Call upon the Lord when life is at its worst, not just when you feel your best.

SAMSON: STAY CONNECTED TO THE SOURCE

Our list of biblical meteorologists wouldn't be complete without at least one rainmaker. Samson was incredibly good at making his own atmosphere. The problem is that he created the wrong kind of weather. Rather than changing his atmosphere from negative to positive, Samson seems to have had a gift for making hailstorms appear from a sunny sky. He was driven by his violent passions like a ship battered by contrary winds. Jealousy, anger, lust, rage—everything he felt pulled him further away from God and His purpose. You can read his entire story in Judges 13–16.

Samson is perhaps best remembered for his ill-fated romance with Delilah. Remember though, Delilah didn't control Samson's strength or steal it. She merely disconnected him from it. She became the object Samson pursued instead of God's will. As a result, he lost the great gift God had given him and is known as one of the most tragic figures in all of Scripture.

Ironically, Samson's great strength was his undoing. He had such physical prowess that he was constantly tempted to rely on that strength to solve his problems. If he was angry, he could muscle his way to victory. When he was surprised, he could react with instant fury. Strong emotions such as anger or excitement always tempt us to believe that we have the force, will, or energy to handle our circumstances on our own. Often when we think of someone swayed by emotion, we are thinking of a person who is moody, sad, or fearful. People who are subject to more active emotions like rage, hatred, or spite can be equally unstable in their walk with God. Beware the temptation to rely on the power of your negative emotions. As with Samson, they will lead you wrong every time.

To avoid being tossed around by your emotions, you must do what Samson failed to do: remain connected with your source of strength. When driven by fear or anger, push back by reaffirming what you know to be true. Commit the promises of God's Word to memory and recite them when you are anxious or afraid. Run to your Father in prayer when you are frustrated or discouraged. When angry, stop. Don't allow strong emotions to disconnect you from your source of strength and stability, your relationship with your heavenly Father. And remain connected with your fellow believers in Christ. Your connection to the body of Christ, the church, is a great source of strength and stability. The fellowship of the church can keep you level during tumultuous times.

CLEAR AIR

To create your own atmosphere, you must learn to master your emotions. Feeling high or low does not change the power of God to deliver His people. Faith is not a feeling; it is an acceptance of truth in the face of adverse circumstances. Whether you are on the mountain, in the valley, or even in the pit, you will find over and over in scripture that God's power proved to be equal to the task at hand.

Most of what we have learned from our biblical weathermakers boils down to a simple lesson: to maintain a consistent walk with God, you must have the right attitude about your circumstances. You must examine your motives, your purpose, your emotions and most of all your level of faith to be sure they are centered on God and not selfish outcomes or your own fears. When you are seeking God's kingdom first and have an unshakable faith that He is capable and willing to lead you through the circumstances of your life, however difficult, you will master your emotions and walk consistently with God. Everyone faces a lion in a pit on a snow day at some point. We all have a worst day of our lives. Even then, God is constant. As Paul tells us, "If we believe not, yet he abideth faithful: he cannot deny himself" (2 Timothy 2:13).

With every victory, you will become stronger and more stable in your relationship with God. Remember, you take on the strength of that which you overcome. If you're feeling low, don't despair. The sun has a sinking spell every night, but it comes back up every morning, and the darkest hour is only sixty minutes. If you can handle it, adversity makes you stronger. It also makes you a kinder and more empathetic person.

ROCK: GAINING STABILITY IN AN UNSTABLE WORLD

We've learned something about gaining consistency in your relationship with God by creating your own atmosphere, that is, by filtering negative emotions out of your mind by putting God's agenda ahead of your own, overcoming faith with fear, and remaining connected to your source of strength through prayer, Scripture, and worship. Now let's explore another metaphor for the constancy of God, a rock. Nothing is more stable than bedrock, the solid layer of rock just beneath the surface of the earth. Builders love to get in contact with bedrock because they know that when they do, their structure will be unshakable. Stones in any form are a symbol of stability. To remain stable in your relationship with God, you too need contact with "the Rock."

TRUST GOD, WHO HAS PRECUT THE STONES FOR YOUR LIFE

The writer of 1 Kings tells us that when the builders of Solomon's temple brought the stones to the building site, they were already cut and ready to be placed into the temple structure. Workers in Jerusalem didn't have to cut the stones to size because they were already perfectly shaped. That way, there was no sound of a hammer or chisel to be heard. Everything was pre-made so it would fit together without force.

Many people think that when they come to God's house for worship, they must somehow beat themselves into shape in order to enter in. They seem to believe that they must whip themselves into a frenzy or display some wild emotion or cry an ocean of tears in order to get God's attention. In fact there is no need for that. You do not have to make yourself appear more ready or somehow force God to bless you. His plan for you is precut. His word has already been laid out. His power is already here. You do not have to make God move. You just need to trust what God will do because He is ready to put the stones together and give you a Holy Ghost miracle. Stop seeking the highs that bring you to inevitable lows. Accept that God is at work in your life and has been since before your birth. His plan for you is already laid out; the stones are there, waiting to be assembled. By seeking Him daily in prayer and Scripture, worshiping with His church, and doing His work in the world, you are building a fine spiritual house, one that will delight your heavenly Father.

BASE YOUR LIFE FIRMLY ON CHRIST, YOUR CORNERSTONE

A cornerstone is the most important stone in the construction of a building. In previous times, when buildings were entirely constructed of stone, the cornerstone was the key to the stability of the entire structure. It had to be perfectly cut, perfectly placed, and incredibly strong. As the first stone laid, it was the reference point for the entire building and bore much of the weight. Today, cornerstones are largely ceremonial but still important. The cornerstone is often inscribed with important information such as the date of construction, the name of the builder, or the names of significant benefactors. In a sense, the building still depends on the cornerstone.

Christ is our cornerstone. Jesus said this about Himself, "Did ye never read in the scriptures, The stone which the builders rejected, the same is become the head of the corner: this is the Lord's doing, and it is marvellous in our eyes?" (Matthew 21:42). He is the solid rock upon which we build a stable life. Many people are trying to build their spiritual life based on something other than a solid relationship with God through Jesus Christ. They seek excitement, or miracles, or prosperity, hoping that these things can substitute for the stability of walking with God every day. As a result, their lives are constantly up and down. When good things happen, they claim a blessing from God and are elated. When they face difficulties, they conclude that God has abandoned them. Worst of all, this kind of shifting spirituality leads to personal disaster. Desperate to find some good thing in life, such folk are prone to making poor choices that make their situations even worse. Jesus talked about this exact phenomenon in His parable of the wise and foolish builders. He said:

> *Therefore whosoever heareth these sayings of mine, and doeth them, I will liken him unto a wise man, which built his house upon a rock:*
>
> *And the rain descended, and the floods came, and the winds blew, and beat upon that house; and it fell not: for it was founded upon a rock.*
>
> *And every one that heareth these sayings of mine, and doeth them not, shall be likened unto a foolish man, which built his house upon the sand:*

> *And the rain descended, and the floods came,*
> *and the winds blew, and beat upon that house; and*
> *it fell: and great was the fall of it.*
> (Matthew 7:23-27)

Following the teaching of Jesus does not lead to a storm-free life. However, it does provide the spiritual and emotional stability to withstand the storms that come. Those who base their spirituality and happiness on circumstances, supposed "blessings" from God, prosperity, or any other thing are sure to be disappointed. Anchor your life on Christ by reading the Word, spending time in prayer, and obediently following the direction of the Holy Spirit.

DRAW STRENGTH FROM THE ROCK

The rock is one of the most common metaphors for God in the Old Testament, and it always carries the connotation of stability and strength. David wrote: "The Lord is my rock, and my fortress, and my deliverer; my God, my strength, in whom I will trust" (Psalm 18:2), and Isaiah said, "Trust in the LORD forever, for the LORD, the LORD himself, is the Rock eternal" (Isaiah 26:4 NIV). Key to gaining consistency in your spiritual life is learning to depend on God for help, protection, and strength. Life has too many ups and downs to expect that you can always remain level on your own. You need a source of strength that is outside yourself; you need to depend on the Rock.

Sometimes you take refuge in the Rock through worship. Think of Abraham, who built an altar of stone to make his sacrifice. The Bible says we have an altar, who is Jesus Christ. He's our stone. He's our rock. He's our fortress. When you pray, set all that Christ has done for you right there before you like a stone. Lean on that work of Christ. Lay hold of it. Lay the sacrifice of your life upon it. Take refuge in Christ, the Rock of your salvation.

Sometimes you need the strength and comfort of God when you are confused or troubled. Think of Gideon, when he was trying to figure out if God would work for him in defeating the Midianites. As a test, he brought a meal offering and set it on a rock. Some of us don't have our meal offering on the rock. He made a sacrifice in order to seek God's mind. When you feel God calling you, lay your sacrifice upon the Rock. Demonstrate your faithfulness to God through prayer, through worship, through giving and serving others.

In response to Gideon's sacrifice, the angel of the Lord took a staff, went over and touched the rock. Fire flared from it, consuming the meat and the bread (Judges 6:21). Lay your sacrifice before the Rock and see what He will do with it. Some say there is no power left, that there are no miracles and that God does not move. Most assuredly, power still comes from the Rock! There is power in prayer, in the Word, and through the Spirit. Lay your sacrifice before the Lord and He will answer with power.

There are times when we seek the Lord because we need provision. We say that we have a financial need, but the need is always for something else: food, shelter, medical care, transportation, and so on. When you have a material need, a rock might seem an unlikely source. But the Rock of our salvation is also a source of plenty. Think of Moses in the wilderness. When the people were thirsty, he drew water from a rock by striking it with his staff (Exodus 17:6). Our Rock is the source of all that we need, material as well as spiritual. When you are in need, take refuge in the Rock.

And don't forget the story of David, which we've already mentioned in this chapter. When he faced a giant too large and terrifying to defeat on his own, he selected five smooth stones—though he only needed one. Those stones represent David's unshakable faith in the Rock of Israel. David knew that in any crisis, the best defense is to rely on the God, our refuge and strength. No wonder the psalmist later wrote, "From the end of the earth will I cry unto thee, when my heart is overwhelmed: lead me to the rock that is higher than I" (Psalm 61:2).

Through prayer, through worship, through sacrifice, through faith, depend on the God who never changes. The Barberton Greenstone Belt in South Africa is said to be the oldest mountains in the world. Some scientists estimate their age as 3.6 billion years. Whether they are right or not, I don't know. What I do know is that the Rock of our salvation is eternal. You will gain stability and consistency as you learn to depend on Him.

PRACTICING THE PRINCIPLE OF CONSISTENCY

An old saying describes the difference between an amateur and a professional in any discipline. "Amateurs produce when they feel like it; professionals produce when they don't feel like it." Consistency is important not only in sports or music or academic studies: it is vital for your ongoing relationship with your heavenly Father. What makes the Father dance with delight over you? Certainly He is pleased anytime you seek Him. Yet He must be absolutely thrilled, delighted enough to leap for joy or turn a cartwheel, when you seek Him, trust Him, and rely on Him day after day, week after week, year after year. Are you seeking a more thrilling spiritual life? Don't. Instead, seek a disciplined, constant, daily relationship with your Father. I promise you, He will be pleased.

Consistency: it wins football championships, and separates amateurs from professionals in any discipline.

YOUR NEXT MOVE

Your next move is to gain consistency in your walk with God by identifying and eliminating the ups and downs in your spiritual life. Try one or more of these actions to accomplish this.

1. Ask a trusted friend or mentor, "Where do you see inconsistency in my spiritual life?" Be prepared for an honest answer that will challenge you at a point of weakness, selfishness, or temptation. Do not be defensive, rather ask your friend to help you by pointing out any time when you are behaving inconsistently.

2. Create your own positive spiritual atmosphere by practicing a daily affirmation for the next three weeks. Choose a Bible verse or other positive affirmation to say to yourself each morning and whenever tempted to discouragement. Some possible affirmations are Romans 8:31, Jeremiah 29:11, and Isaiah 41:10.

3. Recall the last time you battled discouragement, dropped out of church, fell into temptation, or experienced some other spiritual low point. Debrief this experience with yourself: What factors led up to it? What relationships,

positive or negative, were a factor? What thoughts and emotions did you experience at the time? What helped you recover? What lessons can you learn from this that will enable you to be more consistent in the future? Share your findings with a trusted friend.

• • • • • • • • • • • • • • • • • • • •

STEP 4
Come into Agreement with the Father
The Principle of Divine Agreement

It's called the football, but it is neither oval in shape nor made of pigskin. It is actually a metal briefcase enclosed in a leather satchel and carried by an armed officer of at least O-4 rank, a major or lieutenant commander. In street terms, this is the President's "go bag," containing everything the commander in chief would need in case of a major national crisis. Inside is a secure satellite phone, a list of secure locations where the President could go for safety, plans for continuity of government, and letters the president signs delegating authority to the vice president should that become necessary. And there is something more. The football also contains a credit-card sized document enclosed in an opaque plastic cover, called the biscuit. A single column printed on the biscuit contains several series of letters and numbers. These cryptic strands are the Gold Codes, which the President could use to initiate a nuclear strike.

We might have an understandable fear about placing so much power in the hands of one person. What if that person—a president or presidential advisor—became unstable and ordered a nuclear strike for malicious or absurd reasons? That concern is considerably lessened by what is known as the two-man rule. This regulation places a fail-safe against a malicious or inadvertent launch. By this doctrine, the President alone cannot authorize a nuclear strike. The Secretary of Defense must confirm the order. When a field commander receives the order, the two-man rule continues to be in effect. For example, both operators of a missile launch crew must agree that the order is valid by comparing the Gold Code against a sealed authenticator, which is stored in a safe with two locks. Each operator holds the only key to one of the locks. After verifying the code, the operators must simultaneously insert the keys into the missile control panel. The key slots are located out of reach from one another so that it is impossible for one person to insert both keys. So in order to launch a nuclear weapon, a minimum of four people must agree that the order to do so was valid.

What happens if just one of the four disagrees? Nothing. The launch order is void without that agreement. And what if they do agree? Within two minutes, one of 450 LGM-30 Minuteman III intercontinental ballistic missiles will rise from its silo, traveling at approximately 15,000 miles per hour toward a target up to 6,000 miles away. Arriving within 24 minutes, the missile will deliver a W62 thermonuclear warhead, creating a blast equivalent to 170,000 tons of TNT, more than ten times the strength of the bomb that destroyed Hiroshima in 1945. When the President, the Secretary of Defense, and two missile operators come to agreement, incredible power is unleashed.

Obviously, we all hope that no such agreement will ever come as regards the release of nuclear weapons. However, the procedure for launching these terrifying arms uncannily mirrors a positive kingdom principle that governs your life, the principle of agreement. In your spiritual life as in national defense, where there is no agreement, nothing happens. Yet when there is agreement between you, the Father's will, and any other believer, tremendous power is unleashed. God, who seems so often to be hiding Himself and withholding His power, comes into full view. When you come into agreement with the Father, anything is possible.

Many Christians live sporadic, unsatisfying, anemic spiritual lives because they have failed to grasp this basic principle. They run from church to church, conference to conference, or from one media preacher to the next hoping to find the secret key that will unlock God's power in their lives. They do not realize that they hold the unique key that will release new peace and power: agreement with God's will.

AGREEMENT WITH GOD

Being in agreement with God is bringing yourself into line with His will and purpose for your life. It is accepting and participating in the Father's plan. God does have a plan for every person's life, including yours. Isaiah teaches us this and gives us a remarkable insight into what that means when he writes, "Woe unto him that striveth with his Maker! Let the potsherd strive with the potsherds of the earth. Shall the clay say to him that fashioneth it, What makest thou? or thy work, He hath no hands? Woe unto him that saith unto his father, What begettest thou? or to the woman, What hast thou brought forth?" (Isaiah 45:9–10). From these verses two things are obvious: one is that God does have a purpose in creating each of us, and the other is that we are often at odds with the purpose. Though we have been made as we are for specific reasons, we may arrogantly think we know best and refuse to accept God's purpose for our lives. This lack of agreement results in powerlessness. We are like missile operators who can't agree that the launch code is valid. As a result, there is no connection with the Father and nothing happens in our lives.

You may have observed this in your own life as you look at the spiritual experiences of others and find yourself envious. "Why didn't God make me more like them?" you wonder. "Why can't I have their gifts or abilities?" Rather than accepting the purpose God has for you, you waste time and energy wishing your life could be more like someone else's, and even questioning God's judgment on the matter!

Returning to the words of Isaiah, we see that a completely different experience is possible, for the prophet continues, "Thus saith the Lord, the Holy One of Israel, and his Maker, Ask me of things to come concerning my sons, and concerning the work of my hands command ye me" (Isaiah 45:11). In other words, when you know what God wants and commit yourself to that end, He will make it happen. David made a similar observation when he said, "Commit thy way unto the Lord; trust also in him; and he shall bring it to pass" (Psalm 37:5). When we are willing to agree with the Father's divine purpose and rejoice that we are given authority to participate, then we are allowed the wonderful privilege to "taste and see that the Lord is good" (Psalm 34:8). This is what we mean by the principle of agreement. To agree with God is to accept His purpose for your life and to experience the divine yes as a result. The Father dances with joy when His children come into agreement with Him.

AGREEMENT IN JESUS' TEACHING

Lest you think the principle of agreement is a doctrine that depends on only one or two obscure verses of Scripture, let's look further to see the overwhelming biblical support for this experience. It is written throughout both Testaments and is especially evident in the teachings of Jesus.

In John 14 we see that Jesus taught this concept to His disciples in preparation for His departure and their ministry. He said, "Verily, verily, I say unto you, He that believeth on me, the works that I do shall he do also; and greater works than these shall he do; because I go unto my Father. And whatsoever ye shall ask in my name, that will I do, that the Father may be glorified in the Son. If ye shall ask any thing in my name, I will do it" (John 14:12–14). When we agree with the Father and His will, we shall have the power to ask anything. Agreement with Christ—through faith in Him and His work—brings this incredible level of favor with the Father.

Jesus also teaches us that this agreement is directly related to our ongoing faithfulness. He says, "If a man abide not in me, he is cast forth as a branch, and is withered; and men gather them, and cast them into the fire, and they are burned. If ye abide in me, and my words abide in you, ye shall ask what ye will, and it shall be done unto you. Herein is my Father glorified, that ye bear much fruit; so shall ye be my disciples. As the Father hath loved me, so have I loved you: continue ye in my love" (John 15:6–9). When we "abide in" Christ by practicing the kingdom principle of agreement, we feel the Father's joy! As a result, we are able to produce results in our own spiritual life and ministry, bringing honor to the Father.

What are the limits of this principle of agreement? There don't seem to be any. When the disciples marveled at the power Jesus had, He let them know that they had access to the same power. He said, "Have faith in God. For verily I say unto you, That whosoever shall say unto this mountain, Be thou removed, and be thou cast into the sea; and shall not doubt in his heart, but shall believe that those things which he saith shall come to pass; he shall have whatsoever he saith. Therefore I say unto you, What things soever ye desire, when ye pray, believe that ye receive them, and ye shall have them" (Mark 11:22–24). When we are in true agreement with the Father, He delights to give us whatever we ask. "I say unto you, Whatsoever ye shall ask the Father in my name, he will give it you" (John 16:23).

CONNECTED FOR A PURPOSE

Sadly, many Christians pervert the meaning of these scriptures by claiming they give us permission to tell God what to do. That simply is not the case. We must come into agreement with God, not He with us. When we are in agreement with the Father, He delights to grant our requests for one reason only: that He may be glorified. We exist to serve His purpose and not the other way around. We agree with the Father when we pray, "Thy kingdom come, thy will be done on earth as it is in heaven." In response to that prayer, literally anything is possible. When God is determined to do something and we agree with God's purpose, His power is then released in us to do that work.

The first aspect of agreement is our agreement with God. When we joyfully accept His will for our lives, indeed, His will for the world, we place ourselves in a position of power. God delights in our agreement and is happy to work through us in amazing ways. There is a second aspect of the kingdom principle of agreement, and to understand that we must remind ourselves of the foundational characteristic of God's character: love.

AGREEMENT WITH OTHERS

The apostle John wrote, "Beloved, let us love one another: for love is of God; and every one that loveth is born of God, and knoweth God. He that loveth not knoweth not God; for God is love. . . . Beloved, if God so loved us, we ought also to love one another" (1 John 4:8, 11). These verses show the necessity of being in agreement not only with our heavenly Father but also with His children, our brothers and sisters. When we love one another, we both follow the command of Jesus and follow His example (John 13:34). When we do that, walking in agreement with our brothers and sisters in Christ, the Father is especially pleased and something very powerful takes place. Let's look at examples of that in Scripture, beginning with the founding of the church at Pentecost as recorded in the early chapters of the book of Acts.

AGREEMENT IN SCRIPTURE

On the day of Pentecost the believers "were all with one accord in one place. And suddenly there came a sound from heaven as of a rushing mighty wind, and it filled all the house where they were sitting. And there appeared unto them cloven tongues like as of fire, and it sat upon each of them. And they were all filled with the Holy Ghost, and began to speak with other tongues, as the Spirit gave them utterance" (Acts 2:1–4). Notice, they were "with one accord." The believers were of one mind. They had united themselves in a common purpose—waiting for the power that Jesus had promised would come through the Holy Spirit so they could carry out His Great Commission (see Acts 1:8). They were in agreement with God and with one another. That's when the Spirit moved. Can you imagine the Father dancing with delight as the Holy Ghost fell upon His children? This was the moment of agreement needed to launch the mission of the church with great power.

Neither this agreement among believers nor the power from the Holy Ghost was easily dissipated. Luke goes on to tell us:

> *And they continued stedfastly in the apostles' doctrine and fellowship, and in breaking of bread, and in prayers. And fear came upon every soul: and many wonders and signs were done by the apostles. And all that believed were together, and had all things common; And sold their possessions and goods, and parted them to all men, as every man had need. And they, continuing daily with one accord in the temple, and breaking bread from house to house, did eat their meat with gladness and singleness of heart, Praising God, and having favour with all the people. And the Lord added to the church daily such as should be saved. (Acts 2:42–47)*

Notice the various levels of agreement among the believers. They agreed in doctrine (the apostle's teaching), in fellowship, in worship and prayer, in finances, and in purpose (singleness of heart). The result? Power. Great signs and wonders were done by the apostles and souls were saved on a daily basis. When believers reach this level of agreement with the Father's purpose and with one another, anything is possible.

This is nothing less than what Jesus had told them earlier. He said, "Verily I say unto you, Whatsoever ye shall bind on earth shall be bound in heaven: and whatsoever ye shall loose on earth shall be loosed in heaven. Again I say unto you, That if two of you shall agree on earth as touching any thing that they shall ask, it shall be done for them of my Father which is in heaven" (Matthew 18:18–19). There is something special about the agreement of believers in the common purpose of the kingdom. The Father is especially delighted to release His power through us when we walk in harmony with one another.

COMING TO AGREEMENT

You don't have to have a majority to have revival. Where two agree touching any one thing, God will do it. All you need is one other person besides yourself to create the proper atmosphere in a church service for effective ministry. One will chase a thousand, and two shall put ten thousand to flight (Deuteronomy 32:30). That one other person can be your spouse, a prayer partner, the pastor, the evangelist or someone in the congregation who possesses a kindred spirit. It doesn't make any difference who it is as long as you agree together on God's purpose.

You don't belong to yourself anymore. God now inhabits your physical body and you must be ready to put Him on display. People should be able to look into the windows of your eyes and see the glowing passion of a red hot love for God's purpose, one that can't be doused by the flood tide of Satanic opposition.

How it must grieve the Father to see the lack of agreement among His children today. It seems that each one of us hankers for that Holy Ghost experience of Pentecost, but we do so as individuals and not as a body. Each of us seems more intent on his or her own spiritual satisfaction than in doing the work of Christ in the world. Remember that these believers were not given the gift of the Holy Ghost, speaking with other tongues, or the ability to perform signs and wonders just to make them feel better. These gifts had a purpose: to bring the kingdom of God here on earth just as it is in heaven. The Spirit's power was released for a purpose.

What is your level of agreement with your brothers and sisters in Christ? To what degree are you "with one accord" in your local church? What about your community? Are you striving for a singleness of heart with your sister congregations as much as possible? The divisions and competition we see among churches today is not merely sad—it is destructive. When we cannot come to agreement on the apostles' teaching, the fellowship, breaking of bread, and prayer, the most basic of Christian practices, we cannot expect the Father to dance with delight over us or to release His power through us.

Yet when we are able to set aside our own selfish aims and cooperate together on kingdom purposes, the Father is pleased to empower us. Just a bit later in the book of Acts we read of another prayer meeting among the early believers. "After they prayed, the place where they were meeting was shaken. And they were all filled with the Holy Spirit and spoke the word of God boldly" (Acts 4:31). When we agree on anything concerning God's kingdom, uniting ourselves with Him and with each other, God will be at work.

BRINGING GOD OUT OF HIDING

The principle of agreement may sound at first as if it gives human beings too much power. Can we really tap into God's power anytime we want to? To return to the analogy of the missile launch, does this give us a key with which we can launch the Holy Spirit whenever we feel like it? To answer that question, let's return to one of the foundational passages on agreement that we've already discussed, Isaiah 45.

Buried in this marvelous passage is a curious verse that presents us with a dilemma, for the prophet declares, "Verily thou art a God that hidest thyself, O God of Israel, the Saviour" (Isaiah 45:15). That is puzzling for a couple of reasons. First, God is omnipresent, which means He is present everywhere at all times. How could He then be hidden? Second, we know that God has chosen to reveal Himself in many ways. As the writer of Hebrews put it, "God, who at sundry times and in divers manners spake in time past unto the fathers by the prophets, Hath in these last days spoken unto us by his Son" (Hebrews 1:1). And Paul wrote to the Romans, "That which may be known of God is manifest in them; for God hath shewed it unto them. For the invisible things of him from the creation of the world are clearly seen, being understood by the things that are made" (Romans 1:19–20). God has revealed Himself through prophets, through the created world, and especially through Jesus Christ. How then can He be hidden? And why would He want to be?

The answer lies in knowing that while God may be ever present, while the Scriptures may always be available, and the created world may be ever speaking of His character, God still does not manifest His glory until certain conditions are met. Remember what Jesus said about speaking in parables. Echoing Isaiah, Jesus said He taught in parables so "that seeing they may see, and not perceive; and hearing they may hear, and not understand; lest at any time they should be converted, and their sins should be forgiven them" (Mark 4:12). God does not reveal Himself in the absence of faith. He does not show Himself to skeptics. He does not give evidence of His power to scoffers—or to those who lack agreement with Him. To them, God seems to be hiding.

The good news is God can be brought out of hiding. To those who are in agreement with Him, God is always available. God does promise to reveal Himself to those who are hungry and desperate for a life changing divine encounter. Our lives have become a black hole, sucking in light, matter and energy, and letting nothing escape. We do not see or experience God because we are so consumed with ourselves—our work, our families, our lives, our problems, our desires, our plans. We are constantly wired into electronic communications, social media, and entertainment. It is no wonder that God often seems to be hiding. He could well be in plain sight but we cannot see Him because of the many distractions in our lives.

We must not allow this. Open up and let God minister His grace to you. Let Him heal your hurt so you can be free again. Has somebody wounded you? A wife, a husband, a minister, or a close friend? You feel like your whole heart is one big bruise. Give God a chance to shine out of your life with forgiveness and I will promise that you will be healed. Put away the distractions, set aside the problems, move beyond the hurts and failures of the past and allow the God who is always there to reveal Himself to you. Jesus said, "For where two or three are gathered together in my name, there am I in the midst of them" (Matthew 18:20).

You don't have to flip a coin to decide whether God is present or not. You don't need to play the lottery to determine whether God wants to work. God is omnipresent, which means He is everywhere at all times. That means He is at the grocery store just like He is at church. And He is looking for those who agree with His purpose and those who will settle their differences to agree with their brother and release the power to do it.

God will reveal Himself when you come into agreement with Him and His purpose for your life. And He will especially reveal Himself when you take the further step of uniting with other believers in one heart and mind. Agreement releases power.

Agreement will bring God out of hiding. You have been given scriptural permission through your agreement to release God to do what He desires to do in your life. All of God's promises are yes in Christ, "For all the promises of God in him are yea, and in him Amen, unto the glory of God by us" (1 Corinthians 1:20). Claim the promises of God in the Word. Recite them. Pray them. Agree with God that He is good and that His love endures forever. Agree that He has made your life for a purpose, and claim that purpose.

Praise will bring God out of hiding. When you praise Him, you magnify Him. So clap your hands and lift up your voice with the shout of triumph. David introduced the handclap to Jewish worship. This was the first time we see this type of expression connected with the sacrifice. The rabbis say that He did this because it reminded Him of chains snapping. He wanted the Jewish people to remember the chains of Egypt snapping as they marched out to victory.

When you come into agreement with God, it isn't that you gain the power to do whatever you please or to make God act on your behalf. Rather, God delights to reveal Himself to those who have faith, who seek Him, who trust Him and accept His plans and purpose for their lives. Is agreement a special key that allows you to control God's power? By no means. It is a way to place yourself in a position to see God, to see Him work, and to be empowered to take part in His great plan for the world.

RELEASING GOD'S POWER

I preached my first revival service in an African-American church in Lake Charles, Louisiana, back in the early 1970s. If you are familiar with African-American worship, you know that the church does not have an "Amen corner." The entire congregation is the Amen corner as each member seems to participate by voicing agreement with the preacher. When I preached something that struck a chord with the congregation, some folk would stand to their feet, wave their handkerchiefs, and sing, "Yes," in reply. Others would shout "Amen" or "Preach it!" or "That's right!" There was a tremendous spirit of agreement in that church, and fifteen people received the Holy Spirit as a result. They said yes to God, and He was pleased to grant His divine yes in return. Could we experience something like that in our churches today?

I am convinced the church today has a greater opportunity than ever before to bear witness to its generation, if we will only come into agreement with the Father and with one another. I want to be a part of this generation's witness, and I pray that you do too. As we practice this principle of agreement, affirming God's purpose for ourselves, uniting with others in pursuing the kingdom, and giving the Spirit absolute freedom, I believe we will see the power of God released in a fresh way. I am not talking about a rash of personal mountaintop experiences but a release of the Holy Spirit as at Pentecost, working in and through the church to produce a great harvest. I see clues to this work of God in Psalm 111.

> *Praise ye the LORD. I will praise the LORD with my whole heart, in the assembly of the upright, and in the congregation.*

The works of the LORD are great, sought out of all them that have pleasure therein.

His work is honourable and glorious: and his righteousness endureth for ever.

He hath made his wonderful works to be remembered: the LORD is gracious and full of compassion.

He hath given meat unto them that fear him: he will ever be mindful of his covenant.

He hath shewed his people the power of his works, that he may give them the heritage of the heathen.

The works of his hands are verity and judgment; all his commandments are sure.

They stand fast for ever and ever, and are done in truth and uprightness.

He sent redemption unto his people: he hath commanded his covenant for ever: holy and reverend is his name.

The fear of the LORD is the beginning of wisdom: a good understanding have all they that do his commandments: his praise endureth for ever.

GOD'S GREAT WORK

In this psalm I see at least three works of God described, and they are revealed during the act of worship—the gathering of the church body. To put yourself into agreement with God and others, there is no better place to be than with the gathered church. This is where God's great works begin.

The reasons you attend church are important. Why you go to church and what you expect to receive there will determine what God does in you. This is the power of expectation: it reveals your vision and your faith. God will not work for a deadbeat church. What is God looking for? God is looking for faith. Scripture says that "without faith it is impossible to please God" (Hebrews 11:6). What you expect and believe you will receive from God is a key to unlocking His great work in you and in the world. Faith is the beginning of agreement.

What do you expect God to do in your church? Think back on the greatest revival you have heard of, whether it be one you personally experienced or read about. Even if it is the revival you read about in the Bible, God can outdo it. Perhaps you are suspicious of people who will say, "Wow, that was the best church service I have ever attended!" And the next year, they will make the same statement about another rally or revival service. Is that being shallow? No. It is simply recognizing that God can outdo Himself.

- God created a man from the dust of the earth.

- God enabled the body of elderly Sarah to bring forth a child.

- God caused the virgin Mary to give birth to our Savior.

- God adopted us into his family through salvation.

- God is going to take away His bride, the church.

God's works are great, and He is not finished with them yet. When you gather with the people of God and agree together on the greatness of God and His purpose for the world, still greater works are possible.

GOD'S POWERFUL WORK

God's work in the world is powerful, and it is done to reveal His glory. Nothing can stop this work, and it will endure forever. Isaiah said, "No weapon that is formed against thee shall prosper; and every tongue that shall rise against thee in judgment thou shalt condemn. This is the heritage of the servants of the LORD, and their righteousness is of me, saith the LORD" (Isaiah 54:17). God will show His power to defend His people and His purpose. God's work is a sure work. This is important to remember when we see God and His work opposed by so many people. The purpose that God calls you to participate in is sure and certain. It will be accomplished. Nothing can stand in the way of this work. As Jesus said to Peter, "upon this rock I will build my church; and the gates of hell shall not prevail against it" (Matthew 16:18). And the writer of Hebrews adds, "So that we may boldly say, The Lord is my helper, and I will not fear what man shall do unto me" (Hebrews 13:6).

GOD'S WONDERFUL WORK

Wonder is in short supply in our world. We have created so many technological marvels that we seldom feel amazement at anything—including the work of God in our lives. But God's work is a wonderful work. When we lose our sense of wonder, we allow agreement with God to slip away from us. When we are no longer awed by what God does, He does nothing. When we do not feel a sense of elation and amazement at the gift of the Spirit, we lose the Spirit. When healing no longer results in praise, we no longer see the ministry of healing take place. To be in agreement with God is to be awed by His presence and power, by His work among us.

Listen to the sense of wonder in the words of Isaiah, "For unto us a child is born, unto us a son is given: and the government shall be upon his shoulder: and his name shall be called Wonderful, Counseller, The mighty God, The everlasting Father, The Prince of Peace. Of the increase of his government and peace there shall be no end, upon the throne of David, and upon his kingdom, to order it, and to establish it with judgment and with justice from henceforth even for ever. The zeal of the LORD of hosts will perform this" (Isaiah 9:6–7).

My wife grew up in Australia where her family had a nanny whom they called Nanna Lil. When Nanna Lil came to Provencal, Louisiana, to visit the church where I pastored at the time, she had a unique way of responding to the sermon. When I made a point she agreed with and that resonated in her spirit she would say, "Marvelous." Before God will ever be counselor, or mighty, or peace, or father to you, He must first be marvelous to you. Until you are awed by His majesty, He will never operate in your life. Recapture your sense of wonder. Wander out under the starry night sky, like Abraham, and try to count the stars. Ponder the marvel of a tiny baby. Think of the fantastic truth that God loved you enough to send His own Son to die on your behalf. Agree with God that His works are marvelous, wonderful, filled with mystery. God will only work in direct proportion to how marvelous He is to you. The Lord will not do one thing that is not first marvelous in your own eyes.

COME TOGETHER

When longing to see God move within His church, I have heard some people say, "When everyone starts worshiping the Lord and praying more, we will have revival," or "If only more people would come to church, maybe the Spirit would move." Consequently, they never experience the work of God in a consistent way. At best it is sporadic. This is because they are waiting for someone else to precipitate the work of God.

Yet the gospel has a built in provision that always works. When we are in agreement with God, His purpose for us and His will in the world, and when we come into agreement with one another, God moves. The Father dances with delight and His kingdom is advanced on earth. Think of the Master's command to the disciples who feared that the crowd of five thousand would go hungry: "You give them something to eat" (Mark 6:37 NIV). The disciples were unable to do so. Why? Because they could not agree that it was possible. Rather than affirming the Master's command, they argued. Jesus said, "He that believeth on me, the works that I do shall he do also; and greater works than these shall he do" (John 14:12). This is the power of agreement.

God is ready and willing to bring His kingdom fully to earth. He desires that His will should be done here, just as it is in heaven. Though He seems at times to be hiding, He is more than willing to reveal Himself to those who believe. Will we see a greater work of God in this generation than we have ever seen? Will we do the "greater things" that Jesus spoke of? Will the earth "be filled with the knowledge of the glory of the LORD, as the waters cover the sea"? (Habakkuk 2:14). Yes, when we agree. And then we will see the Father dance like never before.

YOUR NEXT MOVE

Your next move is to come into agreement with God and others so that the power of the Spirit may be unleashed in your life. To do that, discuss the following questions with members of your church or small group.

1. In what ways am I personally not in agreement with God's purposes? In what ways are we as a church not in agreement with God and His purposes? What is the one point on which God most urgently calls us to agree with Him right now?

2. What is our current level of agreement with one another? On what points do we lack agreement? Why? What are our obstacles to agreement? What would it take to bring us into agreement with one another?

3. What action will I personally take to come into agreement with God? What action will I personally take to come into agreement with others? What action will we take as a church to come into agreement with God and one another? When will we take that action?

STEP 5
Find Joy in the Midst of Battle
The Principle of Divine Joy

It has been said that you can't buy happiness, but you can buy coffee and that's close enough. To a soldier during the American Civil War, that was very close to the truth. Our images of the War Between the States are drawn from novels like *The Red Badge of Courage* and *Gone with the Wind*. We think of the sweeping drama, grand battles, whiskered generals, and galloping cavalry. The Civil War was the great test of a nation, the epic saga of brother against brother. It was a war of noble causes and heroic sacrifices waged by larger-than-life champions like Lincoln and Lee and Grant and Jackson. This was also the bloodiest of our national conflicts, leaving more Americans dead than all subsequent wars combined.

Yet, like all wars, this one was fought by ordinary soldiers, young men from Maine and Mississippi, Alabama and Indiana, farm hands and schoolboys, laborers and shopkeepers, citizen soldiers who left hearth and home to spend their days in the tedium of camp life, drilling, marching, and bivouacking under the open sky, passing days or months in boredom punctuated occasionally by moments of sheer terror. To Billy Yank and Johnny Reb, the war was not so much a struggle for freedom or for states rights as a struggle to survive the monotony of sleeping in a tent and living on a ration of salt pork and hardtack. What was the common soldier's refuge in this predicament? Coffee.

The Army of the Potomac consumed eighty tons of coffee and sugar each week, and Union soldiers received a daily ration of one and a half ounces of the precious brown beans, plus sugar.[15] Powdered or condensed milk was readily available through the sutlers, traveling merchants who served the army camps. This meant that coffee was never in short supply, and Union soldiers imbibed it liberally. They would boil coffee for breakfast, after supper, and at any break during the day. The soldier carried coffee paraphernalia on the outside of his kit for easy accessibility, and the slightest halt in a march would result a gaggle of Union troops huddled over a small fire, brewing up a pot of this golden elixir. The sight was so common that cavalrymen took to calling their flat-footed counterparts "coffee boilers." Yes, camp life was boring and battle terrifying, but at least they had coffee.

Well, the Union soldiers did. Hemmed in by the Union naval blockade, the Confederate infantryman found coffee in short supply and felt the lack keenly. A British officer visiting the southern states in 1863 declared, "The loss of coffee afflicts the Confederates even more than the loss of spirits; and they exercise their ingenuity in devising substitutes, which are not generally very successful."[16] Ground wheat, chestnut, sweet potato, carrot, bar-

---

15. Dorothy Denneen Volo and James M. Volo, *Daily Life in Civil War America*, 2nd. ed. (Santa Barbara, Calif.: Greenwood Press, 2009), 153–155.
16. Sir Arthur James Lyon Fremantle, *Three Months in the Southern States: April, June 1863*, (Mobile: S. H. Goetzel, 1864), 41. http://docsouth.unc.edu/imls/fremantle/fremantle.html.

ley, pea, and chicory root were all tried, but none could match the flavor and satisfaction of the original. What the Confederate soldier did have was tobacco, produced in abundance by plantations throughout the South.[17]

We imagine the Civil War as one long infantry charge, but belligerents often spent days or weeks within sight of each other without doing battle, particularly during a siege. During such breaks in action, Union and Confederate pickets would sometimes be stationed within sight of each other, even within a few yards. It didn't take long for these men at arms, whose daily lives were more alike than not, to discover that each had something the other wanted. Outside Fredericksburg, Virginia, a Confederate soldier passed a note across picket lines that said, "I send you some tobacco and expect some coffee in return. Send me some postage stamps and you will oblige yours Rebel."[18] Before long, informal truces were made nearly every time the two armies were at rest. Coffee was sent south and tobacco north, and both sides traded newspapers. Along the banks of the Rappahannock River, Confederate soldiers constructed small sailboats to trade supplies with their Union counterparts. In another theater, James E. Hall, a soldier in the 31st Virginia Infantry, took part in a truce with Union soldiers on March 23, 1865, in which they exchanged newspapers for coffee. Soon after, "the truce ended and both parties resumed the firing."[19] During the siege of Chattanooga, which resulted in more than 12,000 deaths, pickets conversed with each other across the creek, and some soldiers from opposite armies played cards together in addition to trading supplies.[20]

---

17. Ashley Webb, "Coffee in the Civil War," *Emerging Civil War* blog, September 25, 2014, https://emergingcivilwar.com/2014/09/25/coffee-in-the-civil-war/.
18. Ibid.
19. Hall, James Edmond, ed. Ruth Woods Dayton, *The Diary of a Confederate Soldier*, (Lewisburg: University of Michigan Libraries, 1961), 128. http://babel.hathitrust.org/cgi/pt?id=mdp.39015008191622;view=1up;seq=132
20. Sue Eisenfeld, "Breaks in the Action," *Opinionator* blog, New York Times online, February 7, 2014, http://opinionator.blogs.nytimes.com/2014/02/07/breaks-in-the-action/.

War may be dangerous, terrifying, unpredictable, and even deadly. Yet the soldier's life was somehow made more bearable by the simple pleasures of coffee and conversation. When life is at its worst, it is all the more important to find joy in the battle in any way you can. That simple idea is the essence of our next kingdom principle. To survive, let alone thrive, in the ups and downs of the spiritual conflict we are waging, you must find joy in your daily life, even when your circumstances cause you to struggle. For the heavenly Father delights in those who are able to find joy in their service, even amid difficult times.

THE PRINCIPLE OF JOY IN BATTLE

During a time when I was struggling for a higher level of effectiveness in my ministry, I paid a visit to a man I consider to be a prophet of the Lord. He was the principal for every youth camp I attended as a young person, and I consider him a friend and mentor to this day. His name was T. W. Barnes. "Brother Barnes," I said, "you are as close to God as anyone I know. What would the Lord say to me today?" I was hoping for a word of encouragement.

The grey-haired saint did not hesitate for an instant. He pointed a bony finger in my face and said, "Brian, you don't enjoy the battle any more. You must make up in your mind that every morning you will have to unsheathe your sword and prepare yourself for war, for Satan will never give up. He will never cease to try and take you down. And if you make it to heaven and walk through the pearly gates, listen carefully as they close behind you because you will hear the rat-tat-tat of arrows as he makes his last ditch effort to stop you from realizing God's perfect will." That was not exactly the encouragement I had hoped for, but it opened my eyes to the self-pity that was creeping into my heart. I was indeed in the midst of a battle, and I had lost my sense of joy. I could no longer feel achievement, only failure. I could not see possibilities, only problems. In place of the joy of salvation, I felt only tiredness and loneliness. I needed to recover my sense of joy, my delight in doing the Father's will, and my naïve optimism about what God will do in response to prayer.

Brother Barnes' words might have been lost on me because the challenge before me seemed so overwhelming, but the older man paused, relaxed his features, and said a bit more gently, "Remember this, Brian, for every new level of power you achieve, you must also face a new set of devils more sophisticated than the last. But the same thing that defeated the devil before will defeat him again and again. The same name, the same blood, and the same word works over and over again."

Those words were a turning point for me. Without that advice, my spiritual life and my ministry would have been a series of ups and downs, long periods of boredom and frustration punctuated only occasionally by thrilling victory. From that day forward, I have intentionally practiced the principle of joy in the battle. God cannot do anything through a heart that is discouraged, lacking hope, already defeated. In the midst of the struggle, we must find ways to recapture the hope, faith, and optimism that we had at the beginning. We must find joy in serving our Father, even during the hard times. When we do, we will discover the truth told by the prophet Isaiah: "They that wait upon the LORD shall renew their strength; they shall mount up with wings as eagles; they shall run, and not be weary; and they shall walk, and not faint" (Isaiah 40:31).

This is not to say that we do not struggle. We are in a battle! Life is difficult, we are broken by sin, and we face an enemy determined to frustrate our faith and capture our souls. There will undoubtedly be difficult times in your life and ministry. Yet you can find joy in the midst of battle and that joy will enable you to dwell on a level plain, avoiding the spiritual peaks and valleys that lead inevitably to weariness and despair. To discover some principles for finding joy, we will revisit an unlikely hero from the Old Testament, a man who was very much like us but who also possessed an extraordinary gift.

SAMSON, JESUS, AND YOU

Samson was an exceptional man. He had strength far superior to anyone of his day, which was a gift from God. You may be familiar with his exploits, which sound more like the adventures of a comic-book superhero than a saint (see Judges 13–16). His physical prowess was simply astounding. Yet as strong as Samson may have been in body, he was weak in spirit. He was moody, petty, jealous, and self-indulgent. In short, he was human. Therefore Samson is a representative of each one of us.

We may remember Samson most for his great failure, succumbing to the charms of Delilah, who learned the secret of his great strength and sold Samson to his enemies. That is a story of disappointment. Yet Samson's life is something more than a disappointment. For Samson is also a representative of Christ in many ways. From his miraculous birth to his mighty works to his self-sacrificial death on behalf of his people, Samson's life foreshadows the life of the greater Deliverer who would become the true savior of mankind. Samson also represents Christ. Therefore, we may draw positive lessons from Samson's example as well as negative ones. One of the most intriguing chapters in his colorful life centers on his encounter with a lion on his way to a place called Timnah.

> *Then went Samson down, and his father and his mother, to Timnah, and came to the vineyards of Timnah: and, behold, a young lion roared against him.*
>
> *And the spirit of the LORD came mightily upon him, and he rent him as he would have rent a kid, and he had nothing in his hand: but he told not his father or his mother what he had done.*
>
> *And he went down, and talked with the woman; and she pleased Samson well.*
>
> *And after a time he returned to take her, and he turned aside to see the carcase of the lion: and, behold, there was a swarm of bees and honey in the carcase of the lion.*
>
> *And he took thereof in his hands, and went on eating, and came to his father and mother, and he gave them, and they did eat: but he told not them that he had taken the honey out of the carcase of the lion. (Judges 14:5–9)*

SAMSON AND CHRIST

The biblical writer has given us a powerful image of Samson, bringing honey in his hands and presenting it to his father and mother. Imagine the Israelite hero with a slain lion in the background, standing out in the open road with his hands laden with masses of honeycomb dripping with honey, which he holds out to those he loves most. That would make a fine picture, worthy of the greatest artist.

In that portrait, we see an image of Jesus, the conqueror of death and hell. He has destroyed the lion that roared upon us and upon Him. He has shouted victory over all our foes. His word from the cross, "It is finished," was a cry of triumph, and Christ now stands in the midst of His church with His hands full of the sweetness of salvation, presenting it to all who will receive it. Of them, He says, "These are my brother, and sister, and mother." To each of us who believe in Him, Christ offers the luscious banquet that was made possible only through the grand battle of the cross. He invites us come and eat that we may have our lives sweetened and our hearts filled with joy. In this portrait of Samson, we see our triumphant Lord laden with sweetness, holding it forth to all and inviting them to share in His joy.

SAMSON AND YOU

Remember that Samson also represents you in this story. You too are a victor, an overcomer of sin. You have been made more than a conqueror through the power of Christ. Now you also hold forth the honeycomb, the great joy of salvation that is available to all who believe. You stand like Samson, with arms outstretched, inviting others to join the feast. Like Samson, you will encounter many battles—tests of your faith, of your patience and virtue, of your stamina. As you persevere in them, you will be victorious. As Brother Barnes reminded me, the same name, the same blood, and the same Word works over and over again. As you do battle for the Lord without becoming discouraged or losing hope, you will discover great joy, and your work for Christ will be effective.

Samson was a conqueror and comforter, slaying lions and distributing sweetness. So was Jesus. And so are you.

FINDING JOY

Sometime later, Samson composed a riddle based on this episode: "And he said unto them, Out of the eater came forth meat, and out of the strong came forth sweetness" (Judges 14:14). Riddles are things that happen in life that we can't explain. Though nearly everything about this incident and its aftermath is tragic, Samson at least was able to see the irony in the fact that his battle with the lion, which could well have resulted in him being eaten, had produced something to satisfy his own sweet tooth. In doing so, he discovered the principle of joy in the battle. It is possible to find delight in life and ministry, no matter how difficult the circumstances. Let's explore this incident further and learn important lessons for finding joy during the most difficult times.

EXPECT CONFLICT

Samson didn't face the lion until he came to the vineyard at Timnah, which in Hebrew means "an assigned portion." So long as Samson was satisfied to stay home, in the comfort of the Judean hills, living among his family and friends, he was safe. When he stepped out, he found trouble. Interestingly, Samson's parents discouraged him from going to Timnah. They wanted to keep him closer to home. Yet, as the biblical writer tells us, "His father and his mother knew not that it was of the LORD" (Judges 14:4). God had a reason for sending Samson to Timnah. Samson had "an assigned portion" given to him by God. The moment he reached that place, the lion roared against him.

To become a Christian is to enlist as a soldier. Never forget that we are engaged in a mission to make disciples of all nations (Matthew 28:19–20), and face an enemy in the principalities, powers, rulers of the darkness of this world, and spiritual wickedness in high places (Ephesians 6:12). We must expect opposition! No battle is won without a fight. It is a grave mistake to assume that because you are born again, filled with the Holy Ghost, and serving your Lord that your life will be free from problems and conflicts. You must expect that when you are doing God's will you will face opposition, sometimes intense opposition.

When you forget that fact, you are certain to become overwhelmed and discouraged by the problems you face. A wise car owner realizes that all vehicles break down eventually and saves a little money for repairs. In the same way, a wise Christian realizes that attacks from the devil are bound to come and stores up a little joy to weather the conflict. Do not be discouraged when tests come; they will only make you stronger. Do not lose hope when it seems that others will not keep the faith; you are called to a narrow road. Wake up every morning fully expecting the enemy will throw obstacles in your path. Then you will never be disappointed to find that he has. Instead, you will know for sure that you are doing something right. Satan doesn't waste his time fighting those who are no threat to him.

To become a believer is to enter upon a pilgrimage, and the road is often rough: the hills are steep, the valleys are dark, giants block the way, and robbers lurk in corners. No cross, no crown; no conflict, no conquest; no sweat, no sweet.

TAKE COMFORT IN YOUR RELATIONSHIP WITH CHRIST

If Samson is our model for finding joy in the battle, then we must expect that conflicts will come early in life and always at our point of weakness. Though we arm ourselves for the battle through faith, prayer, Scripture, and worship, there is no way to fully prepare for war: it is too chaotic and unpredictable. Veteran soldiers are made by war, not just by drilling. You will never know what the fight is like until you are in it.

That was certainly true of Samson. When he encountered the lion, he was not out hunting, armed and ready for the wild beast. He had no weapon, no armor, and he was completely alone. Samson was not looking for a fight; he had gone to Timnah in search of a wife. Yet it was then, when he was weaponless, alone, and unprotected, that "a young lion roared against him." Even in the ancient world, that was not something that happened every day. It was a remarkable and startling occurrence.

You can count on the fact that your battles will come in the same fashion: quickly, unexpectedly, and at the moment when you are least prepared. Satan will not attack you when you are well rested, well fed, and among friends. He is far more likely to strike when you are hungry, tired, and alone. And he will attack at your point of greatest vulnerability, the weakness that you alone know. Human fellowship is exceedingly precious, but there are points in our spiritual conflict in which we cannot expect to receive it. Each person will face passages in life too narrow for walking two abreast. In certain conflicts, we stand alone.

As our constitutions differ, so do our trials. Each individual carries a secret grief or fear or temptation that no friend can fully understand, for every life has both its mystery and its hidden treasure. So do not be shocked or ashamed when the devil hurls temptations at you that appear to be unique. Never think, "What's wrong with me that I would have these thoughts?" or "Normal Christians would never go through this." Every person feels that way at times. Remember, "there hath no temptation taken you but such as is common to man: but God is faithful, who will not suffer you to be tempted above that ye are able; but will with the temptation also make a way to escape, that ye may be able to bear it" (1 Corinthians 10:13). Though you have a burden that you cannot share with others, you can share it with the Lord.

Find joy in the comfort of your Lord and Savior. Do not allow the devil's schemes to throw you into a fog of despair. Recall the joy of your salvation, and remember the words of the apostle Paul, "For the which cause I also suffer these things: nevertheless I am not ashamed: for I know whom I have believed, and am persuaded that he is able to keep that which I have committed unto him against that day" (2 Timothy 1:12). You will be tempted in ways and at times that are extremely difficult for you. Remember that God is faithful, and hold on to the sweetness of your relationship with Him. He will not abandon you, so don't give up on yourself.

DON'T DWELL ON YOUR PROBLEMS

It is highly significant that Samson did not tell anyone where he had found the honey. When he met his parents, he made no mention of the attack by the lion. He was silent about his great victory in ripping the beast apart with his bare hands, and about the bees that had formed a hive in the carcass. He kept the entire incident to himself. That led, of course, to him composing a riddle about the event, a riddle that caused further problems later on (Judges 14:12–20). Samson didn't want to talk about the battle, even though he had won. He just passed around the honey, which was the sweetness or joy that he had found in spite of the conflict.

Many people like to talk about their conflicts. You hear in statements like these: "Well, life is just a trial right now," or "You just don't understand how hard this is. I'm barely making it through," or "I just hope I can survive this next few weeks; I feel like I'm hanging by a thread." They define their lives by their struggles, not their joys. That attitude saps faith like a leaky bucket. It is completely self-defeating. You cannot expect to experience joy in the battle if all you talk about is how tired, lonely, discouraged, stressed, frustrated, upset, hopeless, downhearted, and beaten you are. You must find a way to recover your sense of joy in the midst of battle.

Niccolò Paganini was an Italian violinist and composer, one of the most celebrated musicians of the early nineteenth century. He is considered one of the pillars of modern violin technique. The maestro toured extensively and played in all the major capitals of Europe. According to legend, Paganini was to give a concert before the nobles and royalty of England. He had his violin tuned perfectly, and everything was set. The curtain opened and the master violinist began to play, filling the air with sweet music. Then the unexpected happened: one of his violin strings broke. Being a master of the instrument, the great violinist was unfazed. He didn't stop playing, for a man with his gift could play well even on three strings.

Before long another string broke. Paganini realized he wasn't playing in a village bandstand but standing on stage before the king and queen of England. It was imperative to put on a great performance, so he kept playing on two strings. Then a third string broke! The master was down to a single string; what would he do? The crowd became agitated, wondering how the great violinist would respond. After a moment, however, they realized that this incredible talent was continuing to make beautiful music on only one string of the violin. Not surprisingly, one of Paganini's best-loved compositions is titled "Variations on One String." If you feel like your life is hanging by a single string, don't worry. God can make beautiful music with only that one strand. Do not let stress, busyness, conflicts with others, or any other form of trial cause you to lose your sense of joy. Recall the many times God has done much with little, and imagine what He will do in your life. Disappointments are bound to come; you must carry a little honey with you.

DON'T LET OTHERS DISCOURAGE YOU

It has been suggested that the lion Samson faced in the vineyard had been placed there intentionally. God had commanded the Israelites to leave the four corners of their field open so the widows and the underprivileged could find food to eat. One theory holds that this particular landowner placed a lion in his hedged vineyard to keep such people out. In a similar way, there are certain systems of belief intended to keep you out of the vineyard of God's blessings. You will hear them expressed in statements like these: "The days of the apostles are over, and the gifts they possessed are no longer available," or, "Of course we all sin every day; God's grace brings our forgiveness, but nothing can change our behavior."

These roaring lions have kept many from experiencing the sweet fruit of God's full salvation, and there are many more: peer pressure, cliques, misconceptions, intellectualism, and poor theology, to name a few. Do not allow others to pressure or subtly intimidate you from seeking all that God has for you. When you face conflicts of that type—sometimes even from other well-meaning

Christians who do not accept the victory that God has promised—keep hold of your joy. Don't dwell on negative thoughts. Respond to criticism with a smile. Keep a positive attitude. You will find joy in the battle.

Remember that Samson didn't meet any lions while he was walking on the main road. It was when he got into vineyards of Timnah—close to the fruit—that the attack came. When you stick to the main highway, the broad road that everyone else is traveling, you may have little fear of being attacked. When you get closer to the fruit—the promises of God, the power of the Holy Ghost—then you will meet opposition. Take that as a signal that you are on the right track, and be encouraged. The closer you get to the vineyard, the louder he will roar. But Satan can be defeated by the power you possess in the name of Jesus Christ.

STORE UP SOME JOY

The idea of finding something good to eat in the carcass of a dead animal seems a bit odd, even repugnant. Certainly, some time must have elapsed in order for the flesh to rot away and the bees to build a hive in the remains. Even so, how is it possible to get fresh food from such a place? The answer lies in the unique composition of honey. It is one of the few foods that does not spoil if stored properly. Thanks to its distinctive blend of elements, which includes sugar, high acidity, low moisture, and hydrogen peroxide, honey will last indefinitely. In fact, archaeologists excavating ancient Egyptian toms have found pots of honey, thousands of years old, still preserved.[21] Under the right conditions, honey can last a lifetime.

---

21. Natasha Geiling, "The Science Behind Honey's Eternal Shelf Life," Smithsonian.com, August 22, 2013, http://www.smithsonianmag.com/science-nature/the-science-behind-honeys-eternal-shelf-life-1218690/?no-ist.

Your joy, like Samson's honey, was made to last. Think of the key elements of honey's longevity: high acidity, low moisture, lots of sugar, and some hydrogen peroxide. Acid and hydrogen peroxide are lethal to the bacteria that would cause honey to spoil, and moisture, necessary for the growth of bacteria, is low. If carefully sealed, those elements ensure that only the sweetness remains.

Is it possible that the reason your joy disappears in the heat of battle is that it lacks the right ingredients, or that it is not stored properly? Keep your joy fresh by creating the right conditions. Kill off the bacteria of anger, resentment, and despair. Keep a low-moisture environment by avoiding self-pity, a special temptation for those facing trials. Seal yourself against negative thinking by choosing friends and associates wisely. Spend time among God's people, drawing strength from their fellowship. The joy of your salvation should last you a lifetime. Store up that joy, for you will surely need to rely on it often in the heat of battle. When Jonathan was weak and exhausted from fighting the Philistines, he found a honeycomb and tasted a little of the sweet syrup. His "eyes brightened" immediately (1 Samuel 14:27 NIV). When you can find even a little joy during difficult times, it will brighten your spirits too.

SHARE THE JOY

Solomon wrote, "Thy lips, O my spouse, drop as the honeycomb: honey and milk are under thy tongue; and the smell of thy garments is like the smell of Lebanon" (Song of Solomon 4:11). Sharing your joy through words of encouragement is one of the surest ways to preserve your happiness in the midst of battle. Again, Solomon writes, "Death and life are in the power of the tongue; and they that love it shall eat the fruit thereof" (Proverbs 18:21).

Some people win the victory but they lose their sweetness. But bitterness should never be the result of battle. Just as Samson had no sooner tasted of the honey than he carried a portion of it to his father and mother, so we should be eager to share the joy of salvation with others. When we do, that same deep sense of peace and well-being will be renewed in us. The best way to do that is by offering words of affirmation, encouragement, and invitation to others. Encourage your friends and coworkers when you feel in need of encouragement. You will both feel better. Affirm others for their faith and strength of character, even when you are struggling. Most of all, invite others to experience the joy you have found through your new life with Jesus. Enlisting soldiers in our battle for souls is a great morale booster.

Notice how eager Samson was to share the goodness he had found. If I were to give honey to my father and mother, I would wrap it up nicely. I might put it in an attractive jar with a ribbon around it, or serve it in as respectable a dish as our kitchen would afford. Not so with Samson. He went to his parents gripping the comb, freshly torn from the lion's carcass, honey dripping down his fingers and forearms. Do you have that same level of eagerness and unselfconsciousness in sharing your joy?

Perhaps you think, "I don't have the right training or techniques to share my good news with others." Better to share the gospel untrained than not at all. Don't wait until you have mastered the technique; simply tell others what God has done for you and let your joy be evident. You will gain as much from the experience as your hearer will, for this will rekindle your joy in the Lord in the midst of life's tough battles. Carry the honey in your hands, even though it drips all round. No harm will come from that, and there are always people hoping for even one drop of good news.

ENJOY THE SWEETNESS

Let's go back and learn the answer to Samson's riddle. He posed it this way: "Out of the eater came forth meat, and out of the strong came forth sweetness." And the answer? "What is sweeter than honey? And what is stronger than a lion?" (Judges 14:14, 18). There is a double sweetness in this answer. First, Samson was victorious over the lion. In fact, it wasn't even a contest. He tore it apart with his bare hands. Even for Samson, a mighty man accustomed to winning great battles, that victory must have been especially sweet. Second, of course, was the honey. This was the icing on the cake, so to speak. The unexpected double benefit of winning the battle. Though the riddle led to even more conflict, we can still picture Samson's joy in composing it, doubly pleased at the fruit of this victory.

Like Samson, you have already won a great victory over "the lion" who seeks to destroy you. Christ won that victory for you on the cross. It is finished. And it wasn't even a contest. Jesus rose from the dead, thoroughly defeating the powers of death and darkness. Though we do fight on during this lifetime, we know that our home in heaven is assured. You have won the battle, and you will win many more—by serving Christ effectively, by overcoming temptation, by showing Christ's love to others. Yes, it is a struggle, but it is one you will win. Take joy in that!

And remember that we are not always fighting battles. There are times when we, like Samson, can pause to enjoy the sweetness of this victorious life in Christ. We don't face down a lion every single day; sometimes we get to eat the honey. The same Lord who bids us, "Watch ye, stand fast in the faith, quit you like men, be strong" (1 Corinthians 16:13) also says, "Rejoice in the Lord always: and again I say, Rejoice" (Philippians 4:4). There is a time to fight, and there is a time to celebrate; a time to do battle, and a time to enjoy the fruits of victory. Allow yourself time to pause and reflect. Withdraw from the fray long enough to see the progress you have made and celebrate the victories you have won. Enjoy the good days that God gives you. Yes, you will return to the front at some point. But that shouldn't prevent you from taking delight in a day of victory, the love of your family, the fellowship of Christian friends, or even the simple pleasure of coffee and conversation.

THE TOOTHLESS LION

It is vital that you learn to practice the principle of joy in the battle. Here's why: if you are unable to find delight in life, even when it is hopelessly tedious or terrifyingly threatening, you will inevitably succumb to despair. Your spiritual existence will be a series of ups and downs, long days of trudging through the valley of boredom, frustration, and failure, punctuated only occasionally by flashes of spiritual victory. You cannot live that way and hope to be a satisfied Christian, let alone a warrior in Christ's kingdom. To live a victorious life, you must expect and accept the difficulties that come with following Christ, yet find joy, peace, and delight even during the hardest times.

The apostle Peter must have been familiar with the story of Samson. Perhaps he had it in mind when he wrote, "Be sober, be vigilant; because your adversary the devil, as a roaring lion, walketh about, seeking whom he may devour" (1 Peter 5:8). This is sound advice. We know that we are engaged in a great conflict and there are bound to be stresses, pressures, and problems in our lives. We live in the heat of battle. Yet a zoologist will tell you something interesting about lions. Old lions have dental problems, just like people do. When these mighty cats lose their teeth, they also lose their bite. So in order to assert their superiority as the king of the beasts, toothless lions tend to roar a lot. These tired old giants sleep most of the day, but when they get up all they do is growl and grumble because they don't have the power to do anything else.

Take that image into battle with you—the toothless lion. While we dare not underestimate the strength and prowess of our enemy the devil, we know that he has already been defeated; his destruction is sure. Thomas More wrote of the devil, "the proud spirit cannot endure to be mocked."[22] When you find joy in the midst of battle, when you refuse to cower in the face of the enemy or give up and bow out of the fight, you remind that toothless lion he is already done for. I can't think of anything that would bring the Father more delight.

YOUR NEXT MOVE

Your next move is to become a person who experiences joy regardless of the circumstances you face. To do that, commit yourself to taking at least one of the following actions.

1. Identify your joy killers and rob them of power. Name the circumstances, conflicts, people, or situations in your life that cause you to feel discouraged. State the reason these things bother you as they do (for example, "He makes me feel powerless" or "It robs me of hope"). Now that you see this connection clearly, break it by asserting God's control over your life in every circumstance.

---

22. Thomas More, *Dialogue of Comfort Against Tribulation: With Modifications to Obsolete Language* (Auckland, New Zealand: The Floating Press, 2013), 72.

2. Cultivate a simple pleasure. As coffee provided some respite for Civil War soldiers, you may find a simple pleasure that refreshes your spirit and enables you to journey on. It might be a hobby like gardening or reading, a form of physical exercise such as walking or cycling, or camaraderie with a friend or fellow believer. Devote time to such restorative activities, for they provide spiritual benefits as well as physical and relational ones.

3. Count your blessings. Despite whatever circumstances you may now face, you can undoubtedly name many blessings in your life. While we often think of blessings only as material things, widen your thinking to include relational and spiritual blessings as well. What has God provided for you? Salvation, health, family, friendships—create your own list.

STEP 6
Praise at All Times
The Principle of Alleluia Attitude

At 7:34 a.m., less than an hour after sunrise on April 24, 1990, STS-31 streaked into the cloudless blue sky above the Kennedy Space Center on Cape Canaveral, Florida. This was the launch of Space Shuttle Discovery on its tenth mission, a special assignment to deploy a telescope that would capture images of the heavens from beyond the earth's atmosphere. This was to be a revolution in astronomy, allowing scientists finally to peer into the furthest reaches of outer space, free from the pollution of manmade light, smog, clouds, particles of dust, and even the air itself. It would be the fulfillment of Galileo's dream, to see more, farther, deeper into the nature of our world.[23]

When the orbital vehicle, as the shuttle itself is known, reached nearly 18,000 miles per hour, the two solid rocket boosters and then the massive external fuel tank dropped away, and *Discovery*

---

[23]. Information on the Hubble Space Telescope and Space Shuttle *Discovery* is available from the National Aeronautics and Space Administration at http://www.nasa.gov/mission_pages/hubble/story/index.html and https://airandspace.si.edu/explore-and-learn/topics/discovery/about.cfm.

settled into low orbit approximately 347 miles above the surface of the earth. The crew of five, led by Commander Loren Shriver, were undoubtedly grateful that their mission was on track. This flight had been delayed nearly five years by the explosion of Space Shuttle *Challenger*. So far, so good.

One day later, April 25, *Discovery's* three mission specialists successfully deployed the 43.5-foot-long, 24,500-pound cylindrical device into orbit, inclined at 28.5 degrees to the equator and revolving around the earth once every 95 minutes. Four days later, at approximately 8:50 a.m. on April 29, *Discovery* glided gently to a stop on the Runway 22 at Edwards Air Force Base near Rosamond, California, having completed its journey of over two million miles in just five days, one hour, and sixteen minutes. The mission was a complete success and mercifully free from the technical failures that had haunted the National Aeronautics and Space Administration in the wake of the *Challenger* disaster.

About three weeks passed, during which the telescope's ground controllers verified the operation of its operating systems in preparation for use. The massive scope's six nickel-hydrogen batteries were charged by twin twenty-five-foot solar panels. The pointing mechanism, capable of locking onto a target without deviating more than the width of a human hair as seen at a distance of one mile, was tested. Finally, on May 20, 1990, with the entire world watching and waiting, the device's 94.5-inch, 1,825-pound main mirror was directed at Star Cluster NGC 3532, and the Hubble Space Telescope transmitted its first image to earth.

But there was a problem. Over the next several weeks, scientists noted that, while most of the images were somewhat better than those achieved by earth-based telescopes, the quality was far lower than expected. Rather than being crisp and clear, the pictures were slightly fuzzy and distorted, as if the lens was out of focus. Analyses of the flawed photos revealed the problem. The Hubble's massive main mirror, likely the most precisely figured piece of optical equipment ever created, was slightly out of shape. At its perimeter, the mirror was too flat by 2.2 millionths of a meter. That's a little more than eight one hundred thousandths of an inch, or about one tenth the width of a strand of hair. The telescope named for Edwin Hubble, whose work was instrumental in forming the Big Bang Theory, was a big bust, a two-and-a-half-billion-dollar waste of taxpayer money. Why? Because the edge of the primary viewing device was 2.2 microns out of place.

Where you stand determines what you see. If you stand on a crowded city street, lit by streetlights and lying beneath a blanket of smog, you cannot hope to see the heavens. If you stand on a mountaintop in the New Mexico desert, far from human habitation and beneath a clear, cloudless night sky, you will see more clearly. If you could stand above the earth's atmosphere as a space traveler does, free from the polluting effects of the atmosphere, you would have the best view of all. Yet, as the Hubble telescope reminds us, even there, the tiniest variation in your vantage point can make a world of difference. Where you stand determines what you see, which is another way of saying that perspective is everything.

What is true in astrophysics is also true in your spiritual life. Having a right perspective is the key to seeing clearly, and seeing clearly is the key to having a mature, growing, stable relationship with your heavenly Father. Many of us are like amateur astronomers in our relationship with the Lord. We observe the sky with a pair of binoculars, and sometimes the view is simply amazing; other times, it is obscured by clouds and streetlights and the instability of our own shaky hands. When we base our thoughts and feelings on whether there are clouds in our lives or whether we are currently standing on a mountaintop or in a valley, our relationship with God will be inconsistent. To see clearly, we must get beyond the pollution of personal circumstances and gain a new vantage point, one that is solid, clear, accurate, and steady. We must learn to see things with absolute clarity, as God sees them. This is the divine principle of the Alleluia Attitude. When you have the proper perspective on God, yourself, and the world, you will have an attitude of praise, which delights the Father.

If an Alleluia Attitude doesn't currently describe your life, it will be encouraging to learn that your perspective can change. Three and a half years after scientists discovered problems with the Hubble Space Telescope a corrective mission was launched. Seven astronauts aboard Space Shuttle Endeavor installed a new main camera and a corrective optics package on the telescope during an eleven-day mission in December 1993. Once the telescope was able to see clearly, so to speak, it began to return images of incredible accuracy and beauty: distant galaxies, giant clouds of rarified gas and dust, planets, moons, giant stars—all in fantastically brilliant color. These breathtaking images are so stunning that they are certain to elicit a word of praise from even the dourest cynic. With a changed perspective, you, too, will see both the Lord and yourself more clearly and colorfully than ever before, and you will praise Him with a glad heart. Let's learn how to adopt an Alleluia Attitude and break free from the inconsistent relationship with God that can mire us in doubt and cynicism.

A GLIMPSE INTO THE HEAVENS

An Alleluia Attitude is a positive attitude about God, yourself, and your circumstances that results from having a proper view of the world. You may already have learned the truth that Chuck Swindoll shared on the subject of attitude: "Words can never adequately convey the incredible impact of our attitude toward life. The longer I live the more convinced I become that life is 10 percent what happens to you and 90 percent how we respond to it. . . . This may shock you, but I believe the single most significant decision I can make on a day-to-day basis is my choice of attitude. It is more important than my past, my education, my bankroll, my success or failures, fame or pain, what other people think of me or say about me, my circumstances, or my position. . . . When my attitude is right, there's no barrier too high, no valley too deep, no dream too extreme, no challenge too great for me."[24] In nearly any area of life, attitude makes all the difference.

What you may not realize is that your perspective determines your attitude. How you react to and interpret your circumstances, including your relationship with God, depends on your point of view. The Alleluia Attitude is based on a proper perspective of the world; it comes from seeing things as God sees them. When you see things only from your own perspective, limited by your negative experiences, the people around you, and even your own health and emotions, you will have trouble maintaining a consistently positive attitude. As a result, your spiritual life also will be up and down—and mostly down. However, when you can gain a divine perspective, a positive attitude will follow. You will reap the benefit in a more consistent, positive, daily experience of God.

A change in your vantage point will certainly make a change in your attitude. It's like the old cartoon depicting a man trapped on a tiny desert island. He is dressed in rags, half starved, and disheveled. This poor fellow sees something on the distant horizon

---

24. Charles R. Swindoll, *Strengthening Your Grip: How to be Grounded in a Chaotic World*, rev. ed. (Brentwood, Tenn.: Worthy Publishing, 2015), 227.

and eagerly shouts, "Boat! Boat!" The next frame shows the same scene from a different perspective. The man in the tiny boat is also dressed in rags, half starved, and disheveled in appearance. He is eagerly shouting, "Land! Land!" No matter how difficult or desperate your life may seem, it will appear different if you are able to have a change of perspective.

To gain an Alleluia Attitude, you must begin to see what God sees. There is no better place from which to gain that perspective than the book of Revelation. Reading Revelation is like peering through the Hubble Space Telescope to get a better look in to the heavens. John the Revelator was granted the opportunity to see beyond this world and into the next. He tells us, "After this I looked, and, behold, a door was opened in heaven" (Revelation 4:1). As we stand at John's shoulder and look through that door, we catch a glimpse of reality that is even more brilliant and colorful than any telescope could capture. Though much about John's vision remains a mystery to human observers, three things appear with amazing clarity, and these three images form the bedrock of the Alleluia Attitude.

A CONQUERING KING

John writes, "And I saw heaven opened, and behold a white horse; and he that sat upon him was called Faithful and True, and in righteousness he doth judge and make war" (Revelation 19:11). The Revelation is replete with images of Jesus that communicate strength, power, and victory. From the outset of the vision, where Jesus is pictured as "one like unto the Son of man" with blazing eyes, a voice like running waters, and a tongue like a two-edged sword (Revelation 1:12–16), we see that Jesus is in complete control of time and eternity. As our King, He wages war on sin and Satan, so that "through death he might destroy him that had the power of death, that is, the devil; And deliver them who through fear of death were all their lifetime subject to bondage" (Hebrews 12:14–15).

Our conquering King rode into death, separating His soul from His body as a warrior unsheathes a sword, to do battle. He emerged victorious over death and the grave. Our King now rules over the armies of heaven and the forces of the world, directing and governing all things. Very soon He will finally triumph over all His enemies. An Alleluia Attitude begins with this perspective of Christ: He is our risen conqueror, in complete control of the past, present, and future. His will shall be done.

When you look at the world and even your own future with doubt, it is difficult to feel confidence in God, seek Him through prayer, and praise Him. When your point of view is that the world is bad and getting worse, you will always have trouble keeping a positive attitude and a positive relationship with the Father. However, when you have complete confidence that the end of the story has already been written, that Christ is indeed victorious, and that if God is for us no one can stand against us, you will cling tightly to your heavenly Father, your source of hope. Your perspective on Christ and His work will make all the difference.

A DEFEATED DEVIL

A second vivid image from the Revelation is the view of Satan as a defeated foe. As with Jesus, Satan is pictured in various ways in Revelation. Perhaps the most vivid portrayal, and certainly the most definitive, is found in Revelation 20:1–3. John writes, "And I saw an angel come down from heaven, having the key of the bottomless pit and a great chain in his hand. And he laid hold on the dragon, that old serpent, which is the Devil, and Satan, and bound him a thousand years, And cast him into the bottomless pit, and shut him up, and set a seal upon him, that he should deceive the nations no more, till the thousand years should be fulfilled: and after that he must be loosed a little season."

To be sure, the Revelation contains many mysterious images and references that leave us with more questions than answers. However, the depiction of Satan's ultimate destruction is as clear as the noonday sun. Satan is a defeated foe, dangerous to be sure because he has been badly wounded, but still a hopeless adversary. Jesus has triumphed over Satan. His place in hell is as assured as is our place in heaven. As Revelation 20 indicates, Satan has yet some little time to work mischief on the earth. Like a wounded animal, he is vicious and desperate, yet he cannot prevail.

An Alleluia Attitude depends on recognizing this reality. No matter how dark the sky may appear, no storm has the power to alter your future. Satan's hold on this world is temporary and incomplete. His grip has already been broken. When we fail to see that, we give Satan too much credit and Christ too little. When we stand in the depths of sin, we cannot see hope of victory. Temptation seems too powerful. Failure seems inevitable. We can easily succumb to a defeatist attitude that says, "What's the use? I'm only human. I will just have to accept things as they are."

An Alleluia Attitude says, "No! Satan is defeated, Jesus Christ is victorious, and I can live in victory with Him!" When you see that the devil's power, however strong, is both temporary and limited, you will have confidence that the Holy Ghost will finish His work in you. No defeat, however discouraging, will seem final. You will constantly run back to your heavenly Father's arms for forgiveness, encouragement, and the strength and power to gain victory.

A VICTORIOUS BRIDE

John is not the first biblical writer to use the image of the bride to describe the church and her relationship with Christ. Paul did so in Ephesians 5, where he focused on the sacrificial love of Christ for the church and her purity. John adds to the metaphor the one thing every great romance demands: an ending in which the bride and groom live happily ever after. "And I saw a new heaven and a new earth: for the first heaven and the first earth were passed away; and there was no more sea. And I John saw the holy city, new Jerusalem, coming down from God out of heaven, prepared as a bride adorned for her husband. And I heard a great voice out of heaven saying, Behold, the tabernacle of God is with men, and he will dwell with them, and they shall be his people, and God himself shall be with them, and be their God" (Revelation 21:1–3).

This is the last and most exciting of the photos captured by John's heavenly telescope, for this is a picture of our future home, where we live happily ever after with Christ. The story ends with the bride of Christ emerging pure and triumphant from the conflict and chaos of time into a radiant and peaceful eternity. Our home is with Christ, and there we will dwell forever, untouched by the evils that now characterize so much of our existence.

This is the third powerful reality that underlies an Alleluia Attitude. When you are able to separate yourself from your conflicts, temptations, and problems so that you can stand in the clear and look, even for an moment, into the future that has been secured for you by Christ, your attitude will be changed from despair to hope, from fear to excitement, from resignation to certainty. When you are unsure of the future and your place in it, the temptation to give up will be ever present. Yet when you have the witness of the Spirit that you are indeed a child of God, loved by the Father, you will have confidence about both your relationship with Him and your own potential. You do not have to wonder if Jesus will love you until the end. He has already promised that He will (John 6:37–39). You are forgiven, you are loved, and you are free. When you see yourself as God sees you, your relationship with Him will shift from one of anxiety, wondering, and feelings of guilt or inadequacy to a relationship based on love. At that moment, you will see that the Father dances with joy over you, both over your present forgiveness for sin and your future reunion with Him in heaven.

THE FOUR ALLELUIAS

The Hubble Space Telescope has captured many spectacular images of the heavens. "Pillars of Creation" is a photo that appears more like expressionist art than hard science. This striking picture of the Eagle Nebula, a vast star-forming part of the galaxy some 6,500 light years from earth, gives the suggestion of human life rising up from dusty clay and set against a cobalt sky. Cat's Eye Nebula comprises eleven rings of cerulean and fuchsia-colored gas and dust that look exactly like the eye of a monstrous feline. Crab Nebula is the remnant of a supernova explosion that is some thirty-six trillion miles wide. Giant strands of apricot, ginger, and golden colored gas surround a sky blue, sea foam, and rose center to create the appearance of a large, and very angry, sea creature. These images are truly stunning. Yet the purpose of the Hubble is not to impress. It is to gather data that can help scientists better understand the nature and workings of God's amazing creation. If the images did not produce a change in our understanding of the world, then the telescope would remain a two-and-a-half-billion-dollar boondoggle. It must produce some result in our lives in order to have value.

Likewise, gaining a heavenly perspective is not a merely intellectual exercise. We do not move into a position to see the world as God sees it so we can say, "Well, isn't that nice?" The point is to gain new understanding that leads to a change in our attitude and ultimately, our relationship with the heavenly Father. Your change in perspective must produce a change in you.

The word *alleluia* is a version of the Hebrew word *hallelujah*. We use this word so frequently as an expression of thanksgiving or delight that we probably think little about its origin. *Hallelujah* is conjunction of two words, *hallal* and *jah*, with the connective letter u to join them. *Hallal* is an imperative, meaning to praise with all your might—physically and spiritually. Jah simply means God. So hallelujah means "Praise God!" This is not a mere exclamation of gladness but a command. When you move far enough away from your own vantage point to see the world from God's point of view, you will be moved to praise God. This attitude will affect all parts of your life, from your intellect to your emotions to your relationships to your behavior. It will transform your relationship with God, and you will find that it transforms you as well. Let's examine four results of this Alleluia Attitude, represented by the four alleluias found in Revelation 19:

> *And after these things I heard a great voice of much people in heaven, saying, Alleluia; Salvation, and glory, and honour, and power, unto the Lord our God:*
>
> *For true and righteous are his judgments: for he hath judged the great whore, which did corrupt the*

> earth with her fornication, and hath avenged the blood of his servants at her hand.
>
> And again they said, Alleluia, And her smoke rose up for ever and ever.
>
> And the four and twenty elders and the four beasts fell down and worshipped God that sat on the throne, saying, Amen; Alleluia.
>
> And a voice came out of the throne, saying, Praise our God, all ye his servants, and ye that fear him, both small and great.
>
> And I heard as it were the voice of a great multitude, and as the voice of many waters, and as the voice of mighty thunderings, saying, Alleluia: for the Lord God omnipotent reigneth.
>
> Let us be glad and rejoice, and give honour to him: for the marriage of the Lamb is come, and his wife hath made herself ready.

You may be on a barren island like Patmos as John was, yet when you begin to see things from God's point of view a great shift happens. Even in a barren place, you will experience a remarkable change of attitude, thought, and behavior. These four alleluias will come to characterize your life.

TRANSFORMATION

Alleluia means praise, but in a more specific sense the first alleluia begins with praise to God for who He is and what He has done: "Salvation, and Glory, and honour, and power, unto the Lord our God" (Revelation 19:1). Getting a glimpse of the world from God's perspective gives you an attitude of hope and confidence. You are able to see what God has done, what He is doing, and what He will do in the future. God saves. He is a rescuer by nature. He has a heart for broken helpless people, and he is moved to help them. What a beautiful thing! God is the source of salvation, and He is therefore worthy of our deepest and most sincere praise.

The result of this alleluia in your life will be transformation. When you realize how marvelous God is and how much He has done for you, it will change your entire life. You will, as Paul put it, "yield yourselves unto God, as those that are alive from the dead, and your members as instruments of righteousness unto God" (Romans 6:13). When you clearly see how much God has done for you, it will change your attitude about Him. You will no longer be tempted to see your heavenly Father as a snarling judge, hoping to find you doing something out of line. You will forever see Him as the heavenly Father who loved you enough to save you and welcome you home. As a result, you will be motivated to honor Him in return. Your entire life will be a song of praise to God.

CONFIDENCE

The second alleluia begins with the recognition of Christ's victory over evil. John writes, "For true and righteous are his judgments: for he hath judged the great whore, which did corrupt the earth with her fornication, and hath avenged the blood of his servants at her hand. And again they said, Alleluia, And her smoke rose up for ever and ever" (Revelation 19:2–3). Here is another gripping image of the demise of Satan and all that he represents. His destruction is represented by burning, with smoke rising up forever and ever. God is just. Evil will be eternally punished. Righteousness will be eternally rewarded. And that gives us confidence to do the right thing, even when it seems difficult or risky.

Many Christians live defeated and discouraged lives, unwilling to step out and try anything for God. They are held prisoner by their own sins, unable to gain victory in a personal sense. And they are held captive by fear—fear of failure, fear of persecution, fear of poverty, fear of ridicule. Yet we serve a victorious King who has defeated our enemy. We should have the confidence to step out and attempt big things for God, or even the small things that now seem daunting to us.

An Alleluia Attitude is based on victory, and that victory leads to confidence. When you see things as God does, you will be willing to claim victory over sin and not be perpetually defeated by the mistakes of your past. When you have this Alleluia Attitude, you will say yes to God's call on your life, even if that means changing your own plans for the future. You will be generous with others concerning your time, your money, and your hospitality because you realize that God is capable of taking care of His own. Nothing is impossible for Him. Your new perspective will bring a deep sense of confidence in God, and that will be evident in your relationships, your finances, your career, and your ministry. An old maxim urges that you should work like you don't need the money, love like you've never been hurt, and dance like nobody's watching. An Alleluia Attitude gives you the confidence to do all three. I have learned from speaking to cancer survivors that those who have beaten this dread disease no longer hear the sound tick, tock, tick when they listen to a clock. To them it says, live, every, moment. An Alleluia Attitude makes you eager to seize the day and the possibilities it brings.

OBEDIENCE

The third alleluia of Revelation 19 acknowledges the throne of God: His Lordship and His sovereignty. This alleluia leads to the Christian act of worship, which is to humbly offer oneself to God. This alleluia releases a word from the throne of God. "And the four and twenty elders and the four beasts fell down and worshipped God that sat on the throne, saying, Amen; Alleluia" (Revelation 19:4). The elders fell facedown before the Lord because they recognized His sovereignty over the world and themselves. This act of worship was a way of saying, "I'm all yours. You'll get no challenge from me; I will do whatever you say!"

Seeing God for who He is, the creator and ruler of the universe, is a humbling thing. It is impossible to maintain an attitude of pride when you have that perspective. The natural result in your life will be an attitude of worship, which leads to obedience and service. Because you know that God is God and you are not, you are willing to place yourself at His service. This was exactly the experience of Isaiah, who was moved by his vision of God first to humble himself and then to volunteer to serve (see Isaiah 6:1–6). This is similar to Jesus' act of worship in Gethsemane, where He said, "Not my will, but thine, be done" (Luke 22:42). And Paul identifies this kind of humble offering of ourselves to God as our true act of worship: "I beseech you therefore, brethren, by the mercies of God, that ye present your bodies a living sacrifice, holy, acceptable unto God, which is your reasonable service" (Romans 12:1).

When you have a right perspective on God, you will have an attitude of humility. That will produce obedience and service in your life. If you are still asking questions like, "Why should I have to give up (a sin you enjoy)?" or "Why should I sacrifice my money or time for kingdom work?" then you have not yet achieved a proper perspective on who God is. When you are in awe of His power and humbled to be in His presence, you will do as Abraham did, as Isaiah did, and Peter, and the twenty-four elders and so many others: you will bow before Him and say, "What can I do to serve you?"

Pride, arrogance, self-promotion, an unwilling spirit—these are contrary to the Alleluia Attitude. Can you imagine a parent dancing with delight over a child who throws a tantrum every time he is asked to clean his room? Yet the Father does dance over those who delight to do His will.

POWER

The fourth alleluia declares, "Alleluia: for the Lord God omnipotent reigneth" (Revelation 19:6). This alleluia acknowledges God's power and releases that power on behalf of the church, His bride. This allows the church to receive everything that Christ has made possible for her. It is an alleluia of possibility, and that produces great joy and anticipation in us.

Many Christians live dull, colorless lives because their knowledge of God's power is just that—knowledge. It has not been translated into experience. They remind me of the story about the ducks who went to church. Perhaps you've heard it. Every Sunday the ducks would waddle out of their houses and down the street to the duck church. There, they would waddle inside and take a seat in their duck pews. The duck pastor would get up to lead them in worship, and he would wax eloquent about the joys of duck flight. "Brothers and sisters," he would shout, "We are ducks, and we were born to fly! We have wings! We can take flight and soar above the earth!"

The duck congregation would erupt with shouts of "Amen!" and dozens of them would get up from their duck pews, flap their wings, and fly all around the duck sanctuary. And then the clock would strike noon, and the duck preacher would pronounce the benediction, and all the ducks would waddle out of church, waddle down the street, and waddle back into their homes.

Many of us believe that the Holy Ghost has the power to transform our lives, elevate our experience of God, cleanse our hearts from sin, and empower us beyond imagination. Yet we do not experience it in everyday life. An Alleluia Attitude allows you to go beyond thinking about the riches we have in Christ to actually experiencing them. Victory over sin, effective ministry, giftedness through the Holy Spirit, a deep sense of joy in life, anticipation for the future—all of this begins with a right perspective on God and His tremendous power to subdue all things to Himself. When you have an Alleluia Attitude, you are able to experience God's power in your life. If you are living a dull, underpowered Christian life, allow your perspective to change your attitude—and your experience. Take hold of the joy, freedom, and power that are yours through Christ. Do not wait for some future day to shed the power of sin and rise up to minister in Jesus' name. You were born to fly!

A CAUTIONARY TALE: THE SPIES IN CANAAN

It is important that you understand just what is at stake in this matter of perspective. So far, we have seen the results of having the right perspective. When you change your vantage point so you are able to see the world as God sees it, you will have a transformed attitude. That new attitude will produce marvelous results in your life—transformation, confidence, obedience, and power.

A change in perspective will revolutionize your relationships with God. However, the opposite is true as well. Having the wrong perspective will produce a negative attitude that bears bitter fruit in your life. That wrong perspective will cause your relationship with the Father to turn sour, and the results will be devastating. Numbers 13 records one of the most tragic cases of a flawed perspective, that of the twelve spies who entered Canaan.

Each of the men chosen to spy out the Promised Land was a man of renown. All were leaders, one from each of the twelve Israelite tribes. Each man was recognized by his peers as worthy of honor. These men would be the first to see and explore the land that God had promised to Abraham and his descendants so long ago. They would be the first Israelites since Jacob to actually lay eyes on Canaan. This select group of men would search out the land and bring back a report to the nation.

Moses instructed these twelve men to go into the Promised Land and see what the land was like—whether the people were strong or weak, few or many. What kind of land would they live in? Was it good for farming or tending herds? Were the cities fortified? What would be involved in conquering the land? The spies were instructed to bring back some of the fruit of the land as a taste of what was to come. They would provide a perspective on the upcoming campaign for the entire Israelite people.

What these twelve men did not know was this was to be a test of their perspective of God and His promises. It was a test of their outlook on life. For it would be their perspective, and not the promise of God, that would determine the people's destiny. God's promise had already been given, and it was inviolable. However, the people's response to that promise would determine whether or not they would see its fulfillment. And that response would depend on their perspective, their point of view, their attitude, toward the Promised Land and the challenges it presented.

These men did not realize the importance of the challenge they faced, but few of us do. We seldom recognize a test of perspective when it comes to us, otherwise we would certainly keep the right attitude. The challenge is to keep the right perspective at all times, even when you are unprepared for a challenge.

After experiencing the Promised Land, a place filled with abundance, for some forty days, the men brought back their report. They did acknowledge that the land was rich and bountiful, but that was not the focus of their description: They said:

> *We came unto the land whither thou sentest us, and surely it floweth with milk and honey; and this is the fruit of it.*
>
> *Nevertheless the people be strong that dwell in the land, and the cities are walled, and very great: and moreover we saw the children of Anak there. . . .*
>
> *And they brought up an evil report of the land which they had searched unto the children of Israel, saying, The land, through which we have gone to search it, is a land that eateth up the inhabitants thereof; and all the people that we saw in it are men of a great stature.*
>
> *And there we saw the giants, the sons of Anak, which come of the giants: and we were in our own sight as grasshoppers, and so we were in their sight. (Numbers 13:27–28, 32–33)*

The most telling sentence in the report is the last one: "And we were in our own sight as grasshoppers." The spies went to the land of milk and honey, but all they saw was grasshoppers. They failed in their mission because they had the wrong perspective. Their view of themselves, of the enemy, of the land, and even of God's promise was wrong. They were looking at everything from their position—on the ground, looking up. They viewed the land the way a child views a playground slide while standing at the foot of the ladder—as a huge, impossible, frightening challenge that is far beyond their ability. They saw only problems and no possibilities. They completely forgot about God's promises.

Had the spies been able to see things from God's perspective—from above—their attitude and experience would have been much different. They would have been like a child perched on the top of the slide, anticipating the great ride ahead. They would have seen that with God, all things are possible, and they would have had a positive attitude, an attitude of victory.

Two of the spies, Joshua and Caleb, were able to keep a divine perspective, and they gave a dissenting report. Caleb said, "Let us go up at once, and possess it; for we are well able to overcome it" (Numbers 13:28). This is the same Caleb who, forty-five years later when Joshua was dividing the Promised Land among the twelve tribes, pleaded for one more opportunity to claim God's promise. Caleb said, "As yet I am as strong this day as I was in the day that Moses sent me: as my strength was then, even so is my strength now, for war, both to go out, and to come in. Now therefore give me this mountain, whereof the Lord spake in that day; for thou heardest in that day how the Anakims were there, and that the cities were great and fenced: if so be the Lord will be with me, then I shall be able to drive them out, as the Lord said"

(Joshua 14:11–12). Amazing! At the age of eighty-five, Caleb was still willing to say, in effect, "I don't care if there are giants in the land; let me have a crack at them! With God's help, I will prevail." Now that's an Alleluia Attitude!

However, Joshua and Caleb were overruled by the majority. The result? That entire generation, except for the two faithful spies, was doomed to die in the desert, never entering the Promised Land. Truly, your attitude is everything. If you have a negative attitude based on a wrong perspective of God, yourself, and the world, you will miss God's blessing every time. Your relationship with God will be marked by doubt, distance, and long periods of seeming silence—which are actually the result of your inconsistent walk with Him. Yet if you are able to see things as God does, you will have the confidence, as Caleb did, to rise above the immediate circumstances and take on any challenge. You will enjoy a consistent, close, powerful relationship with the Father. This is the power of perspective. This is the result of an Alleluia Attitude.

THE POWER OF YOUR CHOICE

Here is the most remarkable thing about your attitude: it is completely up to you. You have a choice every day about the attitude you will adopt. You can't change what you have done in the past, and you can't change what will happen to you on any given day. The only thing you do have absolute control over is how you will respond to what comes your way. You have the power to choose your attitude. Will you make the choice to put an Alleluia Attitude to work in your life? Will you change your vantage point so that you are able to see things as God sees them? Will you allow that new knowledge to fill you with hope, confidence, and a sense of possibility? Remember, your knowledge of God isn't meant only to impress you—it's meant to change you. When you make the choice to praise God through hope, confidence, praise, and joy, you will experience a deeper level of intimacy and joy in your relationship with the Father. And your Father will dance, dance, dance with delight over you.

YOUR NEXT MOVE

Your next move is to develop an Alleluia Attitude by learning to see the world as God sees it. To do that, engage in one or more of the following activities.

1. Number a piece of paper from one to twenty. On each line, write something praiseworthy about God. Don't stop until you have named at least twenty things.

2. The four Alleluias of Revelation 19 refer to transformation, confidence, power, and obedience. Choose the area in which your vision of God's work is the weakest. Pray, "Lord, open my eyes to see what you have done in this area." Listen for the Spirit's voice, and write a brief paragraph that summarizes your learning.

3. An Alleluia Attitude springs from an accurate view of God. Using a concordance or an online Bible search tool, find as many verses as you can that include the words "God is." Summarize what you have learned about God.

STEP 7

Love Jesus

The Principle of Divine Love

The 1850s was a time of hope and optimism in the Western world. For Europe and America, this was a decade of progress. In England, Harry Bessemer patented a new method of producing steel that reduced the cost nearly 90 percent, providing the affordable raw material that would accelerate the industrial revolution. In America, the booming steel industry enabled the expansion of railroads, which quickly replaced canals as a faster, more direct form of transportation. Elisha Otis showcased his safety elevator at the New York World's Fair, a device that made for the worry-free conveyance of passengers to upper floors, paving the way for the development of the modern skyscraper. Professor Benjamin Silliman of Yale College devised a way to distill petroleum into its fractional parts, creating gasoline, the fuel that would propel humankind into the next century. The first transatlantic telegraph cable was placed in service, shortening the communication time from Europe to North America from ten days to 1.1 seconds.

Other sciences were burgeoning too. Significant advances were made in epidemiology, anthropology, and astronomy. Darwin published his Origin of Species. Even the world of fashion was on the move: Isaac Singer developed the first commercially successful sewing machine, and the shorter men's jacket supplanted the long coat as the fashion of the day; and an immigrant from Bavaria by the name of Levi Strauss opened a dry goods store in San Francisco that would later become know for selling riveted denim work pants, which would become a staple of the worldwide clothing market.

Perhaps it was the astounding progress of that remarkable decade that prompted young Johann Ficke to make the long journey from Germany to the New World in 1860, settling eventually on a beautiful parcel of land about a mile west of what is now Pleasant Dale, Nebraska.[25] He would take up a new life in America as a frontier homesteader. With discovery and advancement occurring in every aspect of life and culture, certainly this was a time of bright promise for agriculture as well.

The Nebraska frontier was a harsh place, however, and made for an even harsher life. Far removed from the burgeoning industrial cities of the East, homesteaders were left to carve their existence, literally, from the grasslands of the Great Plains. The first dwellings were constructed of sod strips, cut from the dense prairie grass into three-foot lengths and piled up like bricks. Poles were harvested from the willow thickets along the few creek beds, and overlaid with more sod to form a roof. These durable structures were warm and airtight but not waterproof. Homesteaders

---

25. Del Ficke, "A Farm Legacy Letter to My Family," Ficke Cattle Company website, n.d., http://www.fickecattle.com/a-farm-legacy-letter-to-my-family.

lived in the damp earth with rain leaking on their heads through the spring and fall.

To plant the first year's crop, these intrepid pioneers chopped the hard earth and dropped in seed corn, which would sprout amid the prairie grass. Ground buffalo bones made for fertilizer. With luck, the broken ground would soften by the second year to produce a more ample crop. Farming was labor-intensive work, and a large family was a necessity. Everyone worked the fields, including women and children. Neighbors were not a nuisance to be avoided but a requirement for survival. Barn raisings, corn huskings, and quilting bees formed the fabric of a common life. While technology was fast becoming the staple of life in the affluent East, the western pioneer depended on two things for survival: family and community.[26]

Johann Ficke was a successful homesteader, and by 1888 was able to purchase a nearby farm for his son, H. F. Ficke, and his wife, Annette, as a wedding present. There, the younger Ficke carried on the family tradition of farming and ranching, producing four sons and two daughters. Adolph Ficke, H. F. and Annette's elder son, took over the family farm, extending the Nebraska homestead to a third generation.

The Fickes placed great value on family, community, and the frontier tradition of neighboring. Adolph in particular was suspicious of the mechanization of farming and its growing reliance on chemicals. "The day the horses left and the tractor came was the day we replaced community with completion," he would say. His legacy was the firm belief that family, not technology or seed genetics or pesticides, was the key to a farm's survival. The land was a precious resource that must be carefully husbanded and diligently

---

26. Walter Havighurst, "Pioneer Life," *The New Book of Knowledge*. Grolier Online http://nbk.grolier.com/ncpage?tn=/encyc/article.html&id=a2023250-h&type=0ta

worked. The creativity and commitment of the next generation were the only guarantee of success.

The family farm is an increasingly rare feature of the American landscape. After peaking at some 6.8 million farms in 1935, that number was reduced by more than two thirds by 2002. Farmers and ranchers are aging lot, with a median age of fifty-seven. Most retire without a younger family member willing to take on the hard work and uncertainty of the farming enterprise.[27] Millions of farms that were thriving family enterprises for generations have disappeared. Only a comparative handful of Nebraska homesteads continue to exist as working family farms.

The Ficke farm is one of them. Now operated by Adolph's grandson, Del Ficke, on behalf of his mother, Beverly, the Ficke Cattle Company comprises some 7,000 acres of land. Including Del's infant granddaughter, Attley, a seventh generation of Fickes now inhabits the Nebraska prairie. The family enterprise carries on the family tradition, as H. F. Ficke put it, "feeding and raising our animals well so our neighbors can be fed well."[28] The secret to this farm's survival is easy to understand. As Del says, it "begins with my father, Kenneth, who was always putting himself aside so we would have a better life. His secret was . . . a life-long commitment to clearly communicating to all of us how we were the most essential part of keeping the farm going. We were his legacy, not the land and the livestock, but rather the family he loved so much." It is not more powerful machines or more effective pesticides that make the farm succeed. This homestead continues to exist because of a son's desire to know and continue the father's work from generation to generation to generation.

And this brings us to the seventh step in the Father's dance

---

27. "Vanishing farmland: Loss of agricultural space hurts more than the bottom line, *The Denver Post*, April 25, 2010, D-01.
28. Ficke Cattle Company, "Welcome," n.d., http://www.fickecattle.com/.

of delight. For the heavenly Father delights in those who seek to know and follow truth, the truth revealed to us through Jesus Christ. For it is not new spiritual techniques or livelier services or the latest and greatest ways of doing church that ensure our steady and intimate relationship with the Father. It is our devotion to the Master that causes the Father to dance with delight.

DELIGHT IN SEEKING

One of the most powerful principles that has guided my life is this one, which God placed in my spirit when I was just fourteen years old: God delights in those who seek His truth. We see this throughout Scripture, and especially in two key passages, one from the Old Testament and one from the New. "Thus saith the LORD of hosts" the prophet Zechariah tells us, "The fast of the fourth month, and the fast of the fifth, and the fast of the seventh, and the fast of the tenth, shall be to the house of Judah joy and gladness, and cheerful feasts; therefore love the truth and peace" (8:19). And Paul writes, "And with all deceivableness of unrighteousness in them that perish; because they received not the love of the truth, that they might be saved" (2 Thessalonians 2:10). Those who devote themselves to the truth are blessed with joy, and life, and salvation.

What then does it mean to love truth and be devoted to it? We know, of course, that truth is not an abstract idea or even a set of facts. Truth is a person, Jesus Christ. Jesus said, "I am the way, the truth, and the life: no man cometh unto the Father, but by me. . . . I am in the Father, and the Father in me" (John 14:6, 11). If I am to know the Father and learn His ways and do His will, then I must devote myself to the Living Truth. And so from a young age, I have longed for a true revelation of Jesus Christ. Like the great apostle, I long "That I may know him, and the power of his resurrection, and the fellowship of his sufferings, being made conformable unto his death; If by any means I might attain unto the resurrection of the dead" (Philippians 3:10–11).

I want to know Christ in every possible way—to know of Him, to know His thoughts, to know His ways, to know His work. This principle has guided and shaped my life and ministry more than any other. The Father delights in those who love the Lord Jesus Christ with all their heart. As I have practiced this, I have seen multiplied effectiveness in my ministry. The psalmist writes, "Let thy tender mercies come unto me, that I may live: for thy law is my delight" (Psalm 119:77). I have found this to be true: God delights in those who delight in His truth, who delight in Jesus.

EVIDENCE OF TRANSFORMATION

What does it mean to know Christ? Paul has given us a clue in Philippians 3; it is to be made like Jesus in His death and resurrection. To know Christ fully is to die to oneself and be raised to a new life, to become like Christ. It is to keep His commandments (John 14:15), to love as He loves (John 13:34), to think as He thinks (1 Corinthians 2:16). All of that requires a profound transformation of the self—sanctification. And how does this occur? Again, Paul makes this plain for us: "I beseech you therefore, brethren, by the mercies of God, that ye present your bodies a living sacrifice, holy, acceptable unto God, which is your reasonable service. And be not conformed to this world: but be ye transformed by the renewing of your mind, that ye may prove what is that good, and acceptable, and perfect, will of God" (Romans 12:1–2). We come to know Jesus in this deeper, more complete way, not simply by learning more Bible verses or memorizing more facts about His life—helpful as that may be. We come to know Jesus by surrendering ourselves to Him fully so that we may be transformed in mind and spirit. When we do, our lives are transformed and our relationship with the Father achieves a deeper, more consistent quality.

What does that look like? What evidences of this transformation can we expect to see? In short, what does this deeper walk with the Father look like? Paul goes on to describe the qualities of this transformation in the remainder of Romans 12. Here are ten evidences that he identifies. As you see these results increasing in your life, you may be sure that your knowledge of Jesus is growing deeper and your relationship with the Father stronger.

HUMILITY

The essence of sin in our lives is selfishness, and one of the prime signs of our transformation is humility. To be humble is to have a right opinion of yourself, neither higher nor lower than it ought to be. Paul expresses it this way in the sequel to the key verses on sanctification that we have just read: "For I say, through the grace given unto me, to every man that is among you, not to think of himself more highly than he ought to think; but to think soberly, according as God hath dealt to every man the measure of faith" (Romans 12:3).

The second part of this action is "to think soberly." Sobriety is being of sound mind, in one's right mind, and exercising self-control. So to think soberly about yourself is to have a moderate estimation of your own worth and to curb excessive self-ambition.

It is worth noting that the apostle Peter had a rather intemperate opinion of himself when he boldly declared that he would never deny Jesus. When Jesus contradicted that, Peter spoke "the more vehemently, If I should die with thee, I will not deny thee in any wise" (Mark 14:31). If Peter had had a more sober opinion of himself, he would not have spoken "more vehemently."

When you are convinced that you are beyond fault, when you see the sins of others as somehow worse than your own, when you are sure that your opinions about church are the right ones—and perhaps the only right ones—you need to know Christ more fully. A person who truly knows Jesus refrains from judging others too harshly or himself too highly.

MUTUAL SUBMISSION

Humility leads quite naturally to mutual submission for a truly humble person is willing to make himself accountable to others. When you see yourself accurately, soberly, you are able to see others in the same way. When you do, you will recognize that God has called and gifted others just as He has you. They have wisdom, gifts, abilities, and insights that you lack. When you see that, you are seeing things according to the mind of Christ. Paul further writes, "For as we have many members in one body, and all members have not the same office: So we, being many, are one body in Christ, and every one members one of another. Having then gifts differing according to the grace that is given to us, whether prophecy, let us prophesy according to the proportion of faith; Or ministry, let us wait on our ministering: or he that teacheth, on teaching; Or he that exhorteth, on exhortation: he that giveth, let him do it with simplicity; he that ruleth, with diligence; he that sheweth mercy, with cheerfulness" (Romans 12:4–8).

Simplicity is a virtue acquired by those who are free from pretense and hypocrisy. They are sincere, intellectually honest, not self-seeking, open hearted. According to this scripture, those who are transformed by knowing Christ have a sincere respect for others. They will encourage one another without regard for self. They will be generous with praise and willing to accept correction.

And this is a two-way street. No matter what your current life circumstances are, if you have truly been transformed, you will be able to speak life and blessings to those around you. Everyone benefits from this. As Paul elsewhere writes, "Submitting yourselves one to another in the fear of God. . . . That he might sanctify and cleanse it with the washing of water by the word, That he might present it to himself a glorious church, not having spot, or wrinkle, or any such thing; but that it should be holy and without blemish" (Ephesians 5:21, 26–27). When we mutually submit to one another within the church, all of us grow. Therefore, your willingness to accept others, respect their opinions, welcome the gifts God has given them, and place yourself under the accountability of the body is a prime evidence of your sanctification.

SINCERE LOVE

Love may be the most obvious mark of a Christian. Jesus said that we are to love one another as He has loved us. What does that look like? Paul writes, "Let love be without dissimulation. Abhor that which is evil; cleave to that which is good. Be kindly affectioned one to another with brotherly love; in honour preferring one another" (Romans 12:9–10).

It goes without saying that love should be sincere, that is "without dissimulation." Insincere love would seem to be a contradiction in terms. Yet what passes for love among us is not always marked by sincerity; our love is often diluted by the addition of some other motive. We may love others only if they love us in return, or we may love the truth only when it suits our aims, or we may love the church only when it is convenient to do so. What we really have is love plus: Love plus ambition. Love plus personal benefit. Love plus opportunity.

Sincere love is simple, unadulterated love for the sake of the other person. It is a reckless, abandoned form of love. The only way to achieve that kind of love is to hate evil and cling tenaciously to what is good. We see that principle throughout the Scriptures. The psalmist declares, "Ye that love the LORD, hate evil: he preserveth the souls of his saints; he delivereth them out of the hand of the wicked" (Psalm 97:10). And Amos says, "Seek good, and not evil, that ye may live: and so the LORD, the God of hosts, shall be with you, as ye have spoken. Hate the evil, and love the good, and establish judgment in the gate: it may be that the LORD God of hosts will be gracious unto the remnant of Joseph" (Amos 5:14–15).

When your love of Jesus and His ways, His truth, exceeds your love for yourself, your plans, your benefit, and your desires, you will have achieved this pure, simple, sincere kind of love.

DILIGENCE

Paul's next evidence of transformation is a highly practical one. Here we descend from a discussion of more lofty virtues like humility and sincere love to a day-in, day-out working-class kind of virtue: diligence. Paul writes that we should be "not slothful in business; fervent in spirit; serving the Lord" (Romans 12:11). That word business does not have the same meaning that we know today. This is not an exhortation to be shrewd in the marketplace or attentive to your professional life, though those are fine things to do. Paul here means to give your full and complete attention to doing the Lord's work. Do it with haste, earnestness, and diligence. And do it fervently: with passion, intensity, and zeal.

What level of attention do you currently give to your spiritual condition? With what degree of passion do you pursue your relationship with the Father? To know Christ and to be transformed into His likeness is to have a burning passion for the Father and the Father's work.

CONSTANCY

Another aspect of sanctification is living a victorious life, even when the victory is nowhere in sight. The more we know Christ, the more we are able to keep the faith during both good times and bad, just as He did. Paul describes this life as, "Rejoicing in hope; patient in tribulation; continuing instant in prayer" (Romans 12:12).

Jesus' secret weapon for remaining constant and unwavering in His obedience to the Father was prayer. He was well known for slipping away from the crowd, and even from His disciples, to spend extended times in communication with the Father, sometimes all night long. Prayer is a key to your constancy as well. In addition to prayer, each of us must develop a set of spiritual practices that refuel and energize us. Scripture is an obvious next choice, but beyond that, the things that fill us spiritually may vary from person to person. Disciplines like silence, fasting, Sabbath keeping, and hospitality may further your transformation by helping to keep your daily walk with the Father level, even when the terrain of your life is uneven. If you are not familiar with the practice of The Rule of Five, you will benefit from reading about it in my book *Made for More: 7 Proven Strategies for Reaching Your Full Potential*. Isaiah writes, "But they that wait upon the Lord shall renew their strength; they shall mount up with wings as eagles; they shall run, and not be weary; and they shall walk, and not faint" (Isaiah 40:31). Consistent, daily spiritual disciplines make for a consistent spiritual life, a sure sign of ongoing transformation.

GENEROSITY

Generosity is a sixth evidence of sanctification. Paul continues his exhortation to live a transformed life with these words: "Distributing to the necessity of saints" (Romans 12:13). In Paul's day, the social economy worked differently from today. There were no social programs to ensure the care of elderly or disabled people. As a result, the ill, the elderly, widows, and orphans found themselves in a vulnerable, sometimes dangerous, position.

Against that backdrop, Paul identifies a spirit of generosity as a mark of the transformed life. The more we come to know Jesus, the more we are willing to be generous with those who are at a disadvantage. Jesus said that acts of kindness and generosity offered to "one of the least of these my brethren" is offered to Him by proxy (see Matthew 25:31–46).

When we continue to have the attitude that "what's mine is mine" or the mind-set that says there will never be enough, we do not have the mind of Jesus. To know Christ fully is to be open-hearted and open-handed with others—and that includes both those within the church and those in the world!

HOSPITALITY

The concept of hospitality is closely related to generosity, as shown by the way Paul links them in his exhortation to live the transformed life: "Distributing to the necessity of saints; given to hospitality" (Romans 12:13). The writer of Hebrews extends that thought a step further: "Be not forgetful to entertain strangers: for thereby some have entertained angels unawares" (Hebrews 13:2). Once again, remember life in biblical times was much different from today. Clean, affordable, state-inspected motels did not dot every crossroads, eager to welcome weary travelers. There were no state-sanctioned programs for the resettlement of persecuted Christians or refugees. War, famine, natural disaster, or even simple travel could leave a person displaced, without food or shelter or protection. Hospitality was, and is, considered a great virtue in the Middle East.

The writer of Hebrews gives us a peek into the heavenly economy when he points out that angels do in fact walk the earth, and that our acts of kindness to strangers may in fact further God's mission of mercy. How delightful to think that offering assistance to a stranded motorist or providing temporary housing for a single parent could actually bring you into contact with an angel!

When we are willing to overcome our fear of the unknown and drop the veil of privacy that usually surrounds our lives, we benefit both those in need of food or shelter and ourselves. We become richer for entering into the lives of the people whom God wishes to bless. Jesus came into our world as a helpless child and his family was immediately forced to flee for their lives. When you begin to have the mind of Christ, you will see displaced persons in a new light.

GRACE

To be gracious is to offer others something better than what they deserve. A grace period on a bill payment allows a day or two beyond the due date to make payment without penalty. It is gracious not to correct a person who mispronounces your name rather than to embarrass them publicly for a mistake. Grace is overlooking a mistake rather than trying to balance the scales for every little thing.

And grace applies to the larger things in life too. Paul continues his exhortation to the transformed life by saying, "Bless them which persecute you: bless, and curse not" (Romans 12:14). This of course is an echo of Jesus' own teaching in the Sermon on the Mount, "Love your enemies, bless them that curse you, do good to them that hate you, and pray for them which despitefully use you, and persecute you" (Matthew 5:44). Solomon gives his perspective on that concept in the Proverbs, "Rejoice not when thine enemy falleth, and let not thine heart be glad when he stumbleth: Lest the Lord see it, and it displease him, and he turn away his wrath from him" (Proverbs 24:17–18).

Our inclination is to give people exactly what they deserve, to return insult for insult and injury for injury. When we give into that urge, we demonstrate that the Spirit's sanctifying work is not yet complete in us. For when we truly know Jesus, when we have the mind of Christ, we see others in their sin just as God saw us, as wayward children who need help in finding the way home. When you are able to bear an insult, suffer indignity with patience, and even speak well of those who have slandered you, the transformation that God is doing in your heart will be evident for all to see.

FELLOWSHIP

Individualism is both the blessing and the curse of American culture. We are known to be rugged individualists, and that has propelled many to great achievements in sports, business, exploration, and the arts. However, there is a downside to individuality, which is the loss of camaraderie and mutual support that comes from living in community with others. Paul addresses this directly in his exhortation to live the transformed life: "Rejoice with them that do rejoice, and weep with them that weep. Be of the same mind one toward another. Mind not high things, but condescend to men of low estate. Be not wise in your own conceits" (Romans 12:15–16).

The term for this kind of mutual support is fellowship. Fellowship is born from the humility that we have already seen as a characteristic of transformation. When we have the mind of Jesus, we know that we are "in this together" with our brothers and sisters in Christ. None of us has either a private victory or a private pain: we share these things in common, and that makes the journey easier.

When we look at our fellow members of the body either with envy for their achievements or condescension for their failures, we are thinking like rugged individualists and not as members of a true community. When we can laugh with those who laugh—and occasionally laugh at ourselves—and share the sorrows, setbacks, and even financial reverses of our fellow believers, we give evidence of transformation.

RECONCILIATION

Paul tells us that our ministry in the name of Jesus is a ministry of reconciliation (2 Corinthians 5:18). We have been estranged from God, but Jesus made peace for us. We are also estranged from one another, and reconciling people to Christ and to each other is at the heart of Jesus' mission. The problem is that our natural inclination to return insult for injury is very strong.

That's why Paul makes a special point of this tenth evidence of transformation. When we have the mind of Christ, we will go beyond merely tolerating our enemies and "holding our fire." We will take action to be reconciled with them. Paul writes: "Recompense to no man evil for evil. Provide things honest in the sight of all men. If it be possible, as much as lieth in you, live peaceably with all men. Dearly beloved, avenge not yourselves, but rather give place unto wrath: for it is written, Vengeance is mine; I will repay, saith the Lord. Therefore if thine enemy hunger, feed him; if he thirst, give him drink: for in so doing thou shalt heap coals of fire on his head. Be not overcome of evil, but overcome evil with good" (Romans 12:17–19).

There is no place in the transformed life for revenge or getting even. Those who know Christ the best work the hardest to turn enemies into friends. When we allow the viciousness of others to draw us into being vindictive or vengeful, we are "overcome of evil." When we are kind to those who wrong us, offer them grace, pray for them, and even help them, we can overcome evil with good.

To know Jesus is to be changed. When you have a deep hunger to know Christ more fully, to learn His ways, to adopt His mind-set, to carry on His work, you will become more and more like Him. We are transformed by the Word of God—by the Living Word, Jesus Christ.

LOVEST THOU ME?

To know and love Jesus in an ever-deepening way is the key to having a consistent, intimate relationship with God. And there is a flip side. When we do not commit ourselves to knowing Christ and being transformed into His image, we risk not merely missing out on vibrant relationship with God, but something worse—mistaking our love of the church or of social change or of politics or any number of other worthwhile things for a love of God.

The Ficke farm has been successful into a seventh generation because fathers and sons have realized that devotion to family and the family way of life is far more important than any new technology. To forget that is to fail. Two of Jesus' apostles provide us with a vivid illustration of the danger of loving things, even the things of Christ, more than Jesus Himself.

Many have speculated on the motives of Judas Iscariot in betraying Christ. We know that he was prompted by the devil (John 13:2), but what was Judas thinking at the time? Some have supposed that his zeal for Jesus' mission supplanted his love for Christ Himself. It has been suggested that perhaps Judas betrayed Jesus to the Romans in an attempt to precipitate a revolution. Perhaps Judas was so attached to the idea of an earthly kingdom that he lost sight of the heart and teachings of Jesus. The result was Judas' own destruction. How many of Jesus' modern-day followers have succumbed to a similar temptation? It is easy to allow a love for justice or for righteous living or even the Bible itself to replace our love for the Living Word, the Living Truth, the person of Jesus.

Peter provides a more hopeful illustration of this same temptation. At Jesus' arrest, we know that Peter was willing to take up arms for the cause. Did he, like Judas, envision a revolution brought about by force? Whatever he may have been thinking, Peter later denied three times that he even knew Jesus. He ended the night in a pool of bitter tears (Luke 22:62). Yet that was not the end of Peter's story. When he next met Jesus after the resurrection, Jesus posed a simple question to the forlorn disciple: "Lovest thou me more than these?" (John 21:15). More than what? Songwriter Bill Gaither has suggested an answer in the lyrics to his well-known gospel song, "More than fame / More than wealth / More than the world." In other words, Jesus asked Peter whether his devotion to Jesus Himself was stronger than any competing desire. "Do you love me more than the idea of a revolution? More than the thought of becoming great leader? Do you love me more than your own ideas about who I am or what I am doing? Do you truly love me?"

Three times Jesus posed that simple question to Peter: Do you love me? Three times Peter insisted that he did love Christ and Christ alone. Then what? Then Jesus gave the command to put that love into action by continuing the work that the Father had given the Son to do: "Feed my sheep." When we fall in love with our own hopes and dreams, or with our own ideas about who Jesus should be, or with anything other than Christ Himself, the result is something worse than an inconsistent relationship with the Father. The result is destruction. Yet when we are able to set ourselves aside and be wholly devoted to the Son, who is wholly devoted to the Father, we will carry on the great work that Jesus came to do into yet another generation. And the Father will dance with joy. Yes, the Father will dance.

●　●　●　●　●　●　●　●　●　●　●　●　●　●　●　●　●　●

YOUR NEXT MOVE

Your next move is to demonstrate your love for Jesus by submitting yourself fully to Him so that you may be transformed into His likeness. Open yourself to the Spirit's transforming work through simple steps such as these.

1. Identify any area of hidden sin, pride, or stubborn resistance in your heart by asking the Spirit to search you. Spend time in prayer, asking Him to reveal any aspect of your mind, heart, or body that is not fully devoted to Christ.

2. Offer your whole self as a living sacrifice to God. This is a spiritual act of submission that many make at an altar of prayer during public worship services or revival meetings. Others make this sacrifice quietly during their personal time of communion with the Father. The important thing is that you consecrate all you know of yourself to all you know of God. Take time to do this thoughtfully. A hasty vow is easily broken while a deliberate sacrifice holds great meaning.

3. Testify to your love for Christ by telling others about your desire to live a holy life, as He did. Share your resolve with a friend, accountability partner, or your small group.

AFTERWORD

When the disciples returned from their first mission trip with the report demons had been cast out through their ministry, Jesus "rejoiced in spirit" (Luke 10:17–21). The word rejoice in this passage actually means to leap or jump for joy. We do not know for sure that Jesus jumped and shouted, but if Luke's terminology is to be taken literally, Jesus did make some kind of visible expression that let the disciples know how pleased he was.

Jesus danced because his disciples were fulfilling the purpose for which He had come, which was to effect a righteous transfer of power and produce sons and daughters who operated in the same ministry that He did. Jesus gave his disciples power over the enemy, and He declared that he had seen Satan fall from heaven like lightning. We know that this event had already occurred in heaven through the war won by Michael and his angels. It is interesting that Jesus waited until this moment to acknowledge Satan's defeat. Yet once the disciples understood their purpose, recognized their authority, and began to exercise their spiritual prerogative, cities were affected, hell was defeated, and Jesus danced with joy.

Remember too that Jesus cautioned his disciples not to rejoice in the work of their ministry but rather, that their names were written in the Lamb's book of life. I believe that is because our relationship with God is of more value than any works we may perform in His name. Knowing God is greater than working for God. Yes, Jesus gave them power to tread upon serpents and scorpions; yes, Satan fell like lightning from heaven, but when the disciples realized that their connection with the Father held even greater significance, Jesus rejoiced.

I have written this book with the hope that you too will realize your destiny, discover your purpose, and develop a daily walk with God so that we together may dance into the sunset, rejoicing in and bringing joy to our Father in heaven.